THE LAST TRIAL

FRONTISPIECE: *The Sacrifice of Isaac (Isma'il), a single miniature from a manuscript of the Majma'al-tawārikh by Ḥafiz-i Abrū, prepared ca. A. D. 1425 for the library of Bāysunghur, son of Shahrukh. School of Herat, Persia.*

بای اوبست و اوری و اورا روی افکند و کارد برقفای او نهاد وقوله تعالی فلما اسلما و تله للجبین
ی کودک نهاد و قوت کرد و روی ترکارد بالا آمد ابرهیم ازان عجب داشت سر بکفت
عجب میدمتری کارد بالا برکشت برکشت کرد علط کرده باشی نو ابرهیم بار دکرد کارد برقفای
تاکشی از پشت ماورد کوسفندی سفید و چشمهای سیاه وپای و سیاه و سروها
و باستاد و ابرهیم کارد برقفای کودک نهاد این بار زیادت قوت کرد کارد دو شدوهم

به تا خیر میکنی می ترسم که هر دو بترسم شوم جوز ابرهیم کارد راست کرد و باز برکوبی
و دو کفت صدق الرویا ای ابرهیم آن خواب که دیدی راست کردی و نده بجای آوردی ابرهیم
بلرزیدند و کارد را از دستش بیفتاد وجبرئیل کفت الله اکبر الله اکبر ابرهیم جون کبش را بدید کفت
سر راکفت سر برکشید کبر بکر داد سر برخاست وجبرئیل راد بدید لا اکبر که
رخ برجبین آمد اشک این که بعید ضحی کند جبرئیل و ابرهیم و اشمعیل دع و هرکه
زقیامت ابومه سنه تن شفیع او باشند و جبرئیل کوید که آن کبش ابرهیم علیه الس
و اشمعیل قربان کنند کبش بجنت و بدان کوهها برشد و منار نشید و بدان موضع که امر
و سنک انداز ند و کوید ابرهیم سنکی بینداخت از عقب از کو سفند با ستاد ابرهیم فراز نش
این زمان قربان کنند قربان کرد قوله تعالی و فدیناه بذبح عظیم ودنیا و آن کبش
لک رزقی خدا خواست و این سنت و ابرهیم بر ابرهیم ماند سر الله تعالی بر ابرهیم شناکفت قوله تعالی

THE LAST TRIAL

ON THE LEGENDS AND LORE
OF THE COMMAND TO ABRAHAM
TO OFFER ISAAC AS A SACRIFICE:
THE AKEDAH

by SHALOM SPIEGEL

Translated from the Hebrew, with an introduction,
by Judah Goldin

A Jewish Legacy Book

BEHRMAN HOUSE, INC.   *New York*

A JEWISH LEGACY BOOK

Series Editor: Seymour Rossel

This volume has been published with the support of the American Council on Learned Societies, in order to make this important work of scholarship available in an English translation.

The selection from Wilfred Owne's "The Parable of the Old Man and the Young" is from *The Collected Poems of Wilfred Owen*. Copyright © 1963, Chatto & Windus Ltd. Reprinted by permission of New Directions Publication Corporation and Harold Owen.

First BEHRMAN HOUSE edition, 1979
Published by arrangement with Pantheon Books,
a division of Random House, Inc.

Designed by Anthea Lingeman

Originally published in Hebrew under the title
מאגדות העקדה :
פיוט על שחיטת יצחק ותחייתו לר׳ אפרים מבונא

Copyright, 1950, by the Jewish Theological Seminary of America.

Library of Congress Cataloging in Publication Data

Spiegel, Shalom, 1899-
    The last trial.

  (A Jewish legacy book)
  Translation of Me-agadot ha-'akedah.
  Reprint of the ed. published by Pantheon Books, New York.
    "The akedah" by Ephraim ben Jacob of Bonn: p.
    Includes indexes.
    1. Abraham, the patriarch, in the Midrash.
2. Isaac, the patriarch, in the Midrash. I. Ephraim
ben Jacob, of Bonn, 1132-ca. 1200. II. Title.
III. Title: The akedah.
[BM518.18S653 1979]   296.1'4   79-12664
ISBN 0-87441-290-0

Published by Behrman House, Inc.
1261 Broadway, New York NY 10001

MANUFACTURED IN THE UNITED STATES OF AMERICA

CONTENTS

vi   *List of Abbreviations*

vii   *Introduction*

1   THE LAST TRIAL

139   THE AKEDAH

153   *Index of Biblical References*

161   *Index of Midrashic-Talmudic Sages*

LIST OF ABBREVIATIONS

B.	Babylonian Talmud.
Davidson, *Thesaurus*	Israel Davidson, *Thesaurus of Medieval Hebrew Poetry*, New York, 1924-33. 4 vols.
Ginzberg, *Legends*	Louis Ginzberg, *Legends of the Jews*, Philadelphia, 1909 ff. 7 vols.
Habermann	A. M. Habermann, *Sefer Gezerot Ashkenaz we-Sarefat*, Jerusalem, 1945.
HUCA	*Hebrew Union College Annual.*
J.	Jerushalmi, the Palestinian Talmud.
JBL	*Journal of Biblical Literature.*
JQR	*Jewish Quarterly Review.*
M.	Mishnah.
Mann	Jacob Mann, *The Bible as Read and Preached in the Old Synagogue*, Cincinnati, 1940.
MGWJ	*Monatschrift für Geschichte und Wissenschaft des Judentums.*
MhG	Midrash ha-Gadol, ed. M. Margulies, Jerusalem, 1947.
Migne, *P.G.* and *P.L.*	J. P. Migne, *Patrologia Graeca* and *Patrologia Latina* (Patrologiae Cursus Completus), Paris, 1844-66.
NS	A. Neubauer and M. Stern, *Hebräische Berichte über die Judenverfolgungen während der Kreuzzüge*, Berlin, 1892.
PRE	Pirke R. Eliezer.
R.	Rabbi. After the title of a biblical book: Rabba. After Pesikta: Rabbati.
REJ	*Revue des études juives.*
Salfeld	Siegmund Salfeld, *Das Martyrologium des Nürnberger Memorbuches*, Berlin, 1898.
T.	Tosefta.
ZAW	*Zeitschrift für die alttestamentliche Wissenschaft.*
Zunz, *Literatur geschichte*	L. Zunz, *Literaturgeschichte der synagogalen Poesie*, Berlin, 1865.

INTRODUCTION

I

In 1950, corresponding to the year 5710 of the Hebrew calendar, the Jewish Theological Seminary of America published, under the editorship of Professor Saul Lieberman, a Jubilee Volume in celebration of Professor Alexander Marx's seventieth birthday.[1] Professor Marx had served as professor of history and librarian of the Seminary since its refounding in 1903 by Solomon Schechter. The Jubilee Volume appeared in two parts, of 667 pages in English, of 547 pages in Hebrew. There were forty-five contributors from various parts of the United States, England, Central Europe, and Israel. Some of the contributions were of major, even formidable, importance for Judaica studies, and scholars are still drawing on those learned contributions for their continuing researches. Beyond any shadow of doubt, at least on my part, the outstanding study of the *Festschrift* is that by Professor Shalom Spiegel, *Me-Aggadot ha-Akedah*.

As a rule *Festschrift* studies are of a technical nature and are intended almost exclusively for the professional scholar; this is especially true if the language which the scholar uses is other than English or French or German. Immediately on its appearance Spiegel's *Me-Aggadot ha-Akedah* attracted the attention of scholars in the field of Hebrew literature and folklore. What is noteworthy,

[1] *Alexander Marx Jubilee Volume* (New York, 1950).

however, is that soon thereafter many nonscholars, too, who read modern Hebrew learned about the study and were profoundly impressed by its contents and its style. So Spiegel was awarded a Louis La-Med prize for his contribution to Hebrew letters. Furthermore, in two subsequent jubilee volumes,[2] writing again in Hebrew, Spiegel supplemented his *Me-Aggadot ha-Akedah* with additional discussion. Spiegel on the Akedah, therefore, has been no secret. Yet it is no distortion of fact to insist that the study, because it is written in Hebrew, has remained beyond the reach of many and larger circles where it should be known and examined attentively,[3] for it is devoted to a theme and a problem central to Judaism and Christianity. Translation of *Me-Aggadot ha-Akedah* into English is long overdue. The resolution to undertake such an assignment I owe to a program sponsored by the American Council of Learned Societies.[4]

II
How is *Me-Aggadot ha-Akedah* to be described? Theoretically it

---

[2] *Mordecai M. Kaplan Jubilee Volume* (New York, 1953), Hebrew volume, pp. 267-287, and *Jubilee Volume in Honor of Abraham Weiss* (New York, 1964), pp. 553-566.

[3] One study which has drawn heavily on the material collected by Spiegel is G. Vermes, *Scripture and Tradition in Judaism* (Leiden, 1961), pp. 193-227.

[4] The following is part of a notice that appeared in the March 1964 issue of the *Journal of Biblical Literature* (p. 102): "The American Council of Learned Societies invites interested scholars to call to its attention the titles of books in the

humanities and social sciences, written in languages not widely known in this country, that deserve to be published in translation for the use of American scholars. The ACLS has initiated a program devoted to making such works available by sponsoring their translation into English; it will not itself publish them, but it will arrange for their publication.

"Works proposed for translation should be major works of scholarship that are not available in any of the four languages—French, German, Spanish, Italian —that American scholars may be assumed to read without great difficulty."

is intended to serve as a preliminary statement to a twelfth-century poem by a certain Rabbi Ephraim of Bonn, published from manuscript for the first time.[5] We may say, then, that by means of his discussion Spiegel is teaching us how to read the poem and by implication any Hebrew poem, how to recover the ensemble of ideas and images inhabiting the poet's consciousness and sub-consciousness as he wrote his lines. But to characterize this discussion as no more than an introduction would be understatement verging on misrepresentation, even for a poem of 105 lines, even for the first and critical edition and publication of a poem. Sixty-seven tightly printed pages (in the *Alexander Marx Jubilee Volume*, pp. 471-537) introducing a poem that, together with its own introductory note, line-by-line commentary, and critical apparatus, takes up (pp. 538-547) a little more than nine generously-spaced pages! Granted that the commentator is obliged to spell out in detail what the poet expresses compactly or elliptically; but with all due appreciation of Rabbi Ephraim's *Akedah*, most of its lines can surely be understood without a comprehensive survey of the earlier literature.

It may not be altogether unfair to say that in such an approach as that of *Me-Aggadot ha-Akedah* there is something of intellectual play, something of the deep delight taken by a sensitive scholarly mind in following the surprising turns of the poet's imaginativeness and wonder, and of the scholar's own memory and speculation—as a result of encounter with a great idea. To meet the God of whom it was said not once but several times that "He is gracious and

[5] Spiegel's subtitle in the Hebrew original reads: "A *piyyut* (liturgical poem) by R. Ephraim of Bonn on the slaughter of Isaac and his resurrection." In the subject index of his *Thesaurus of Medieval Hebrew Poetry*, Israel Davidson listed eighteen references to Akedah poems, and R. Ephraim's poem is one of them. This poem, along with other poems by R. Ephraim, has now been reprinted by A. M. Habermann in *Studies of the Research Institute for Hebrew Poetry in Jerusalem*, VII (1958).

merciful, slow to anger, and of great kindness, and repenteth Him of the evil" (Joel 2:13),[6] commanding His favorite to offer up as sacrifice that one's beloved son, is sure to produce not only fear and trembling but prolonged reflection. From prolonged reflection on such a theme will come exploration, farther and farther out. The long introduction is probably in part, therefore, the result of the scholar's joy in the long journey demanded by his theme.

But the pleasure in the purely intellectual play of tracing an idea's course will not account adequately for the extent of these "preliminary remarks." True, a poem even on the Akedah—which for all its renown and for all its frequent retelling has never grown dull—can be introduced with greater economy, particularly if one's learning is not exceptional; yet the theme is vaster than the poem, even had the poem been twice or three times its twenty-six stanzas—vaster and deeper reaching too. There is no escaping the multitude of questions raised by the story in the twenty-second chapter of Genesis and the recurring commentaries on it, and uses to which it has been put, in different epochs; for, as a leading recent commentator on Genesis remarked,[7] in the episode of Genesis 22, "The very essence of the biblical process itself is laid bare. . . ." It is no accident that when Erich Auerbach[8] decided to·choose a biblical narrative which would serve as bold contrast to "the genius of the Homeric style," he selected the Akedah story. The story of how God, totally without forewarning, commanded Abraham to offer Isaac as a sacrifice, and then, as the father "put out his hand and picked up the cleaver to slay his son," peremptorily prevented that slaughter, has fixed itself as a permanent preoccupation of the three Book monotheisms. For Moslem tradition the story was significant

[6] See also Jonah 4:2. Compare Psalm 145:8 and Exodus 34:6.
[7] E. A. Speiser, *The Anchor Bible: Genesis*
(New York, 1964), p. 164.
[8] *Mimesis* (Princeton, 1953), ch. I, "Odysseus' Scar."

enough to cause the victim-son to be identified with Ishmael rather than Isaac.[9] In Judaism and Christianity the original cast of characters was retained, the received biblical text was acknowledged as authoritative, and then generation after generation proceeded to read its lines and between its lines. Here mother religion and daughter religion found they each had much at stake. By the middle of the third century of the common era, artists were depicting the story in a synagogue interior. Since that time, in Christian art alone, up to the fifteenth century, it has been a favorite theme: the Index of Christian Art at Princeton gives no less than 1,450 entries for Genesis 22:1-19.[*]

I do not wish to suggest that by his thoroughgoing treatment Spiegel implied there was no more to be said on the subject of the Akedah. Note his title: *Me*-Aggadot ha-Akedah, not *Aggadot* ha-Akedah. He had undertaken to discuss *part* of the lore that had grown up around that great trial, that part—and perhaps even that only partially—germane to the understanding of Rabbi Ephraim's poem. What additional aspects of that lore, for study of the poem, especially for study of the lore itself, still remain to be explored, I would myself be at a loss to indicate: is there anything in the iconographic tradition that should be drawn upon?[10] One thing is certain: Spiegel had best be taken literally, and if he says that in his study he is examining traditions *me-aggadot*, of only part of the Akedah legends and lore, he means just that. If nothing else, those

---

[9] See briefly, however, J. Eisenberg in *Encyclopaedia of Islam*, II, 532b, and A. J. Wensinck, ibid., p. 544.

[*] The earliest representation I know is, of course, the one from the Dura Synagogue (first half of the third cent.). Miss Rosalie B. Green, of the Index of Christian Art, informs me that "for the scene of Abraham sacrificing Isaac" there are ten exam-

ples dated in the second and third cent.
[10] See in this connection the brilliant discussion and notes of M. Schapiro, "The Angel with the Ram in Abraham's Sacrifice: a Parallel in Western and Islamic Art," *Ars Islamica*, X (1943), 137-147 (a study once called to my attention by Spiegel in a conversation having nothing to do with this introduction).

subsequent studies of his, to which I referred above, compel us to take him at his word. The theme is very likely inexhaustible.

III

Even in its biblical version, the story is perplexing. Leaving aside literary problems—for example, the two forms of reference to the deity (God, Lord), or the meaning of specific words and clauses in the text, or the resorting to certain repetitions although the compactness of the chapter is exemplary—the reader cannot help wondering, What purpose was to be served by that sensational test? Could nothing less have demonstrated Abraham's complete faith and absolute obedience? [11] That the earliest readers and students of Genesis should therefore have pondered and pondered over the story is no surprise. When we find, however, that almost two thousand years ago, despite the distinct order "Do not raise your hand against the boy, or do *anything* to him," there was already plainly recorded a notion that the faithful patriarch did lay hand upon the boy, did inflict a wound—and more—on his son, perplexity passes into shock. The most scrupulous custodians of the sacred text, those earliest students dared to fly in the face of the very words they were so painstaking to preserve? When Scripture said, Don't, they dared to contradict? [12]

[11] Cf. the dialogue between God and Satan in the Job-like scene, in Ginzberg, *Legends of the Jews*, I, 272f., V, 248f.

[12] Even when moderns dare, it comes as a shock. Wilfred Owen's "The Parable of the Old Man and the Young" comes to mind:

"*So Abram rose, and clave the wood, and went,*
And took the fire with him, and a knife.
And as they sojourned both of them together,
Isaac the first-born spake and said, My Father,
Behold the preparations, fire and iron,
But where the lamb for this burnt-offering?
Then Abram bound the youth with belts and straps,
And builded parapets and trenches there,
And stretchèd forth the knife to slay his son.

Doubtless even in antiquity and even among the devout, absolute uniformity did not prevail; and one is frequently tempted to assume that even among the strictest of loyalists there is still room for deviation. Perhaps the view that Abraham did something to the lad on the altar was an erratic and fugitive opinion. How, then, shall we explain the persistence of this view, or variants thereof, in generation after generation of some of Israel's most pious souls? And those who repeat this account do so without any sense of the bizarre.

For so radical a departure from the explicit there must be an explanation. So, correctly, all scholars who have dealt with the Akedah traditions have said, and some have sought to locate the explanation in the collision between Christianity and Judaism. As everyone knows, nothing could be more repugnant to the God of Israel than human sacrifice. Even the story of Jephthah hardly qualifies as an exception: considering what must have been his earliest impressions in the first years of his life and the companionship he enjoyed for some time after he was driven from home, his conception of piety has little to instruct us. Whatever the purpose of the trial in Genesis 22, the declaration "Do not raise your hand against the boy, or do anything to him" is unmistakable. No less so the biblical prohibition against offering up of one's seed to any moloch.

When lo! an angel called him out of heaven,
Saying, Lay not thy hand upon the lad,
Neither do anything to him. Behold,
A ram, caught in a thicket by its horns,
Offer the Ram of Pride instead of him.
But the old man would not so, but slew his son,—
And half the seed of Europe, one by one."
The emphasis is mine. (Note, by the way, that Owen calls Isaac the first-born; as for the Ram of Pride, cf. the vision in Daniel 8.) On Owen's last line see the note by Edmund Blunden in *The Poems of Wilfred Owen* (New York, 1931), p. 122; but it may well be that the line is a distinct retort to Genesis 22:16-18, particularly v. 17. The way Benjamin Britten has incorporated this poem into the Offertorium of his *War Requiem*, opus 66, is midrash of the twentieth or any century at the level of genius.

That being the case, the tradition that something was done to Isaac when he lay bound on the altar—certain scholars suggested—must have originated in times when the supreme sacrifice of the Christian messiah was invoked as demonstration that the complete, the perfect act had been enacted only on Golgotha, that the act on Moriah was only a preamble, a partial adumbration of the greater and full one later. And since those who rejected the Gospels refused to be outdone in manifestations of loving God with all heart and soul and being, they appropriated ideas—said these scholars—that were in actuality anathema to the God of the patriarchs and their descendants.

This explanation was rejected by other scholars, and they insisted that these Akedah ideas had already received expression in the Jewish liturgy before Christian influence could be at work.

What then *are* the facts, and on what grounds can they be established? This Spiegel has undertaken to examine carefully, on the basis of ancient texts and institutions. What his researches revealed to him I leave for the reader to find out, as he reads what Spiegel cites and follows Spiegel's fastidious analysis. A wonderful expedition lies ahead where legend behind the legend is disclosed, and legend and history interact, and history and midrash converge.

IV

As though a tradition contradicting the literal but unambiguous heavenly summons to the patriarch were not enough to startle readers of Genesis 22, there occur in Rabbi Ephraim's poem several lines (61-68) that stretch the imagination to breaking point:

> *Down upon him fell the resurrecting dew, and he revived.*
> *(The father) seized him (then) to slaughter him once more.*
> *Scripture, bear witness! Well-grounded is the fact:*
> And the Lord called Abraham, even a second time from heaven.

The ministering angels cried out, terrified:
Even animal victims, were they ever slaughtered twice?
Instantly they made their outcry heard on high,
Lo, Ariels cried out above the earth.

Two slaughterings? And to this *Scripture* bears witness? But never mind Scripture, since an ingenious commentator can extract there's no telling what. What, however, can the statement mean, what possible reality can such a statement reflect or refract? And that the poet intends to be taken seriously is evident, for he insists not only on the testimony of the Holy Scriptures but on something factual and well known, although to be sure he helps himself to an established formula, "well-grounded is the fact," *la-davar raglayim.*

Once again I prefer not to deprive the reader of the excitement of learning, and leave it to him to follow Spiegel's exploration and discovery. The rewards will be not only those of top-flight literary criticism, but the recovery of a historical moment of great consequence.

v

Rabbi Ephraim's interpretation of the biblical Akedah story is admittedly very far-fetched,[18] and it illustrates clearly what happens when the literal meaning of texts is crowded out by the commen-

---

[18] Far-fetched exegesis is of course hardly confined to any one literary or religious tradition, especially when applied to divinely revealed scriptures. Gilbert Crispin, abbot of Westminster (11th century), claimed that since it was impossible to give a literal explanation of Ezekiel 44:2ff., "And the Lord said unto me: This gate shall be shut, it shall not be opened, neither shall any man enter in by it . . . ," inevitably the passage had to be understood spiritually; "the 'shut gate' signified the Virgin, and the words 'neither shall any man enter in by it' meant that the Mother of Christ had known no man before Jesus was conceived and born." (B. Blumenkranz, "The Roman Church and the Jews," in *The*

tator's conviction that the ancient revealed formulation has anticipated every single detail of later events. However, regardless of the
persuasiveness of this or any particular interpretation, that conviction lies at the heart of Midrash all the time: the Scriptures are not
only a record of the past but a prophecy, a foreshadowing and fore-
telling, of what will come to pass. And if that is the case, text and
personal experience are not two autonomous domains. On the contrary, they are reciprocally enlightening: even as the immediate
event helps make the age-old sacred text intelligible, so in turn the
text reveals the fundamental significance of the recent event or
experience.

Thus we find that the story of Abraham and Isaac rises almost
spontaneously in the mind of one generation after another. But
each generation has its own experiences and its own concerns.
These inevitably affect the conception of that story; they also affect
the ways the story is used. At one time, a mother bereaved of her
seven martyred sons will suddenly cry out: Abraham, how can you
compare your trial to mine? At another time, as ideas of atonement,
of merit of the Fathers, of the divine attributes of justice and mercy,
of the role of the righteous slain for His sake, are explored, again
the conduct of the patriarchs is recalled. So too at still other times
when the supreme self-sacrifice is enacted. Ritual practices, whose
roots stretch far back into remote antiquity, even into prehistory,
will be explained in terms borrowed from the patriarchal narrative:
a ram's horn used in worship will be associated with the ram at
the Akedah; if ashes are used in a public fast, they serve as reminders
of him who compared himself to dust and ashes or of him who was
reduced to ashes. Whatever the occasion, a biblical story or a biblical verse is brought into conjunction with it. So constantly past and

World History of the Jewish People: the   New Jersey, 1966), p. 91.
Dark Ages, ed. C. Roth (New Brunswick,

present react to and upon each other, and life is given an order, a coherence, by the themes which govern the Holy Scriptures and the reinterpretations of those themes.

Indeed, as we observe how each age treats the biblical story, we come to appreciate still another possibility: that the biblical account itself may be but the selected, the adopted version of a much more ancient narrative which once upon a time circulated orally and which possibly included elements now no longer in the written record. Can we be sure that such elements have been completely forgotten? Perhaps the biblical author chose to write down not everything he knew but only what seemed fitting to him to record in his time; and what he would not put down in writing, word of mouth and memory might well preserve. Or perhaps he did leave some slight traces of the older narrative in Genesis 22, and we had best reread the chapter.

Be this as it may, by assembling the variety of postbiblical interpretations of the biblical story, *Me-Aggadot ha-Akedah* exhibits what the story of Abraham and Isaac came to mean to successive generations. Simultaneously it reveals that, once having entered the consciousness of their descendants, Abraham and Isaac never go away.

VI

Discussion and exposition of such high order as are represented in the following pages require at least two things, and it will not be amiss to spell these out even at the risk of repeating the presumably obvious.

First of all, enormous learning is required, downright erudition. A theme so central to the nervous system of Judaism and Christianity as the Akedah has proved irresistible to countless and all kinds of teachers and writers, and Spiegel has ignored none of them. He has drawn on all parts of Scripture and Apocrypha, Midrash and Talmud, on Greek, Hebrew, and Latin, Synagogue and Church literature; chronicles, codes, liturgy and ritual, biblical exegesis and homiletical discourses; history, folklore, philosophical reflection from Philo to Kierkegaard, traditional Bible commentary and higher criticism no less. The parade of sources is a lesson to anyone who wishes an example of how to carry out a task undertaken responsibly. And, as Spiegel demonstrates, not even the printed resources will suffice; the manuscripts too must be consulted; what is more, inscriptions from the nonbiblical universe and etymologies recalling the prebiblical world are instructive. Even then we are not yet done: still ahead of us lies the checking and rechecking, the evaluation, of variant readings and alternative versions.

No work like *Me-Aggadot ha-Akedah* could ever have come into existence without an awesome respect for detail—and many a detail and cascades of "cf.s" in footnotes at first sight of seemingly minor significance. Think once more of the nineteenth verse of Genesis 22: "Abraham then returned to his servants, and they departed together for Beer-Sheba." Where was Isaac? the ancients already wondered; with this wonder Spiegel himself starts the discussion, and new planets come into view.

What makes attentiveness to detail (to variant readings and even spellings, to different formulations) particularly mandatory in the study of classical sources of the Akedah (and related motifs) is that for the most part we are not dealing with literary products in the strict sense of the word—though even were that the case, focused attention would still be necessary. What survives in midrashic and talmudic records are mostly fragments and splinters of deliberations, remnants of give-and-take, homilies, anecdotes, lectures. Frequently before one can make out even the lexical meaning of some particular statement, he must piece together the remains of statements scattered over a textual area of no mean limits. And then, the extraordinary associations! What has Passover to do with Abraham? What has Isaac to do with the second verse of the sixth chapter of Hosea? What has Psalm 81:4 to do with Genesis 22:13? What have a king of Moab long after Balak and a Mesopotamian *mantis*[14] to do with the Akedah? Even more: Is there any comparison between the behavior of the patriarchs and that of certain heroes in ancient Greece? for example, between Abraham's son and Agamemnon's daughter? Is there anything relevant to our study in a Latin inscription preserving a fossil Punic term? Above all, what makes Isaac, who rose at last from the ordeal on the altar, the prototype of those whose slaughter was a *fait accompli*?

In this connection, indeed, consider the very word *Akedah*. This noun never occurs in Scripture; only seven times does some form of the verbal root *akad* ('*qd*) occur in the Bible[15] (as a passive participle six times), and all seven of these in Genesis, and six of the seven within only two chapters, 30 and 31, where the term refers to a characteristic of beasts in a flock. Only once does the verb in the active, conjugated form appear, *wa-yaakod*, "and he bound," and that is in our story of the Trial of Abraham and Isaac. I do not believe it has yet turned up in the manuscripts of the literature of the Dead Sea settlements. Further: in the Mishnah the noun *Akedah* does occur, only once, and even then in what might be called a thoroughly neutral sense, as purely descriptive of the manner of tying the Tamid lamb, the lamb for the Perpetual daily offering in the Temple, in preparation for slaughter.[16] But the noun does appear

---

[14] Philo, for example, never calls Balaam *prophetes*, and I believe the same is true of Josephus.

[15] Exclusive of the place-name Beth-eked, which occurs twice in II Kings 10:12, 14. Compare n. 19 below. On the noun *eked*, see Eliezer ben Yehudah, *Thesaurus* (Jerusalem and Tel Aviv, 1950), IX, p. 4670.

[16] On the other hand, in the single occurrence of the noun in the Tosefta (Sotah 6:5), the connection with Isaac is explicit. As to the variant reading in the critical apparatus of the Zuckermandel edition, p. 304, cf. S. Lieberman, *Tosefeth Rishonim*, II (Jerusalem, 1938), p. 61.

in connection with Isaac—to be precise, in connection with Isaac's *blood*, "the blood of Isaac's Akedah"—in the tannaite Midrash, the Mekilta de-Rabbi Ishmael.[17] This seems to be the earliest occurrence of the term in relationship with the experience Isaac had to endure.[18]

And henceforth what do we find? Once any writer or speaker helps himself to that word, an Isaac apparition rises in his mind.[19] Not only that, but more and more the term is employed for scenes and echoes of the acts of *martyrs*. Isaac is the paradigm of whom? Not of the survivor of the ordeal, but of everyone who paid for the Sanctification of the Name with his life.

Nor is this the whole story. There is a time when the Akedah victim in effect says to his persecutor, "I will not yield to your demands; do with me what you please"; and then the tyrant acts. But there come times when in effect the Akedah victim says to his persecutor, "I will not yield to your demands," and even before the persecutor takes action, the victim anticipates him and does away

[17] In the Lauterbach edition (Philadelphia, 1933), I, pp. 57 and 88. But this does not occur in Mekilta de-Rabbi Simeon, ed. Epstein-Melamed (Jerusalem, 1955). In the latter source, however, see R. Joshua's view, p. 4, and Spiegel's comment below, ch. VI.

[18] In the light of this first appearance of the noun, may it be that the noun *akedah*, when used in conjunction with Isaac, was understood *at once* as not just the binding but the actual sacrifice? Note: the *blood* of Isaac's *Akedah*. See below, Spiegel's seventh chapter. And note too the citation from the Yalkut that Spiegel has put as the heading for his second chapter: "attah *akadeta mizbeah* ehad, wa-ani *akadeti* shiveah *mizbehot.*"

It is surely of some significance that the single occurrence of the noun in the Mishnah, in the neutral sense, is in the treatise *Tamid* (4:1), on which see L. Ginzberg, "The Mishnah Tamid, the Oldest Treatise of the Mishnah," in the three issues of the *Journal of Jewish Lore and Philosophy* (Cincinnati, 1919), and especially J. N. Epstein, *Introduction to Tannaitic Literature* [in Hebrew] (Jerusalem and Tel Aviv, 1957), pp. 27ff.

[19] The *Akedat Yitshak* compilation of R. Isaac Arama (1440-1505) is hardly an argument against this contention, for when you begin playing on words in order to include your name in the book-title, fancy is allowed any number of liberties. This way you can prove that Esther and Haman are referred to by name in the Pentateuch. As Hebrew book-titles go, you might easily get the impression that everyone named Elijah had

with himself—by means of anything, and quickly, lest Heaven's Name be desecrated.

However, to return to Spiegel's analysis and synthesis of the literary sources: It would have been impossible to establish the interconnection of isolated statements and of sundry doctrinal teachings without a relentless tracking down and noting of every clue, and without a deep respect for the individuality of the detail. Not only in the recitation of prayer, but in research, a change of consonants can make the difference between a world sustained and a world devastated. One reason *Me-Aggadot ha-Akedah* is so overpowering is that its author honors the fantastic assortment of data that he has assembled. Hence even an important tentative suggestion of his becomes vindicated fact as a result of the chance discovery of a manuscript fragment, now in Cambridge—again, as one might have anticipated, by Spiegel.

Second: Industry will accomplish much, but it can never replace sensitivity, which is in part congenital but in part also the by-product of years and years of refining of discipline and thinking. *Me-Aggadot ha-Akedah* contains a number of stunning observations because of Spiegel's listening capacities. He hears the tones and undertones of the voices behind the written-down sentences in the literary sources, and therefore he concentrates his attention not only on the word but on the sound—and on the silence too. Thus in a votive inscription he could overhear the original intention and rhythm of what was eventually to become a standard formula in a different context altogether. Or again, a medieval document may be drawn up in language thoroughly derivative from a text which by iteration and reiteration may at first seem to provide no more than rhetorical device: and inside such quotation marks, as it were,

---

to have Elijah's Mantle in his literary wardrobe; in Ch. B. Friedberg's *Beth-Eked* [1] *Sepharim* (cf. n. 15 above) there are eighteen entries with the title *Adderet Eliyahu!*

Spiegel discovers the fury and outcry of historical factuality—a discovery, incidentally, that brings him (and thus us too) to the recognition of a fundamental methodological principle of research. A passage in the prophets discloses itself to him[20] as a choral chant in the progress of pilgrims to their sanctuary. Industry alone will not achieve such responsiveness. And if today we are able to hear much of the orchestration of the Akedah theme as it was developed during many generations, we owe it to *Me-Aggadot ha-Akedah*.

VII

There is one more aspect of the work before us which calls for some comment, and that has to do with Spiegel's own literary style. With one possible exception, in our own times I know no one who is Spiegel's equal as virtuoso in *all* the varieties and modes of Hebrew expression, so richly (I almost said, so like Joyce) exemplified in *Me-Aggadot ha-Akedah*. It is the author's own language in the course of exposition which makes the work a distinguished contribution to Hebrew belles-lettres no less than to historical research. Vocabulary, syntax, cadence, transition from quotation to paraphrase, and summary are so employed as not only to present the author's argument but to make audible the idiom of the original sources which nourish his speech. And these sources are anything but of uniform character, for in the course of centuries writers of almost every literary genre were drawn to the Akedah theme. That is why Spiegel has appropriated the biblical word when a biblical tone is required, the midrashic manner when midrashic conversation and exchange must be dominant, the payyetanic flourish when only incantation does justice to the fact that must be acknowledged, the chronicler's

[20] This he had already demonstrated more than thirty years ago in the *Harvard* *Theological Review*, XXVII (1934).

detail where only by recitative can the enormity of the event be indicated. This whole compound he has stamped with his personal seal: that of modern critical investigator for whom the naturalness of voices from the past has not been destroyed. By summoning biblical, midrashic, mishnaic, talmudic, halakic, haggadic, liturgical, exegetical, *and* modern statements and manners of speaking, Spiegel is reporting not only what the sources say but how they say it. As a result, he adds to contemporary Hebrew expression the resonance of the classical sources, and reinforces the uninterrupted continuity of a literary and intellectual tradition from biblical days to our own.

One final observation on the literary aspect of *Me-Aggadot ha-Akedah*. There is a distinctly oral quality in this literary composition. The reader is addressed directly, is summoned personally to consider the problems raised, to attend as the sources speak for themselves and as the scholar-author lists possible reasons for the particular statement. This is actually the way texts have always been studied in Jewish academies of higher learning. Text after text is introduced, one source is placed in close proximity to the next, so that what is primary and original should not be erased, what is typical should be recognized, and what is unique or uncommon should be clear-cut. The student or reader is not proffered the completed results of research at once; instead he is invited to come along and consider step by step a problem in which the master or author is engaged. No condescension, no suggestion that the venture is beyond the powers of the learner and that therefore he is exempt from consulting the basic documents. For subtle textual problems there is seldom a single solution. In short, we are offered the privilege of participating in an activity and we are not treated as passive spectators. I know of no more genuine courtesy that can be shown a student or a reader.

VIII

The present translation is no substitute for the original *Me-Aggadot ha-Akedah*. To have reduced *nekob ozneka ka-afarkeset ha-zu u-shema* to "Let me have your attention," is to murder a precious association. But in a modern scholarly monograph I can do no better; "Lend me your ears," is to call up wrong associations for the present context: whatever it was that happened to Isaac on the altar, one does not come to bury him. To say again and again "the talmudic Sages," where the Hebrew means that but says instinctively again and again, "the Sages of blessed memory," is not only to suppress a particular cadence, but to hush up the affirmation of a value which "of blessed memory" once incorporated [21] and which, by direction more than indirection, reflects what the Sages came to mean to the house of Israel. "Fortunately" hardly equals *hetib immanu ha-mikreh* or *sihek lanu ha-mazzal* unless, possibly, one takes time out to reflect on the literal meaning of "fortunately." To have attempted anything like "Fortune has been kind to us" would have been mimicry. And so with a number of other phrases and clauses and perhaps whole sentences too. But this was the best I could do.

Truth to say, while I was able to submit the translation to Professor Spiegel for checking and for the correction of my errors, he is in no way responsible for this English version. The permission to make this work available in translation he granted with great reluctance: "I wrote it in Hebrew for thus it shaped itself in my thought; in another language it is not quite what I had in mind." These were approximately his words of protest, which I respect,

[21] See in this connection S. Lieberman, *Greek in Jewish Palestine* (New York, 1942), p. 70, n. 23.

but decided finally to ignore, because it was unfair to those who know no Hebrew but would like to learn something about the Akedah. So too the title, *The Last Trial,* he had nothing to do with. The title is itself intended as midrashic comment on the haggadic statement that God put Abraham to the test ten times and in all of them he proved steadfast.[22]

Regardless of the merits and demerits of the translation, I did strive to capture the flavor and movement as well as the solid matter of this beautiful work. The few departures from the printed text are based on revisions supplied to me by Professor Spiegel.

After preparing rhymed versions of the poetry quoted in the body of *Me-Aggadot ha-Akedah,* I decided finally to abandon them in favor of more literal translation. The line-by-line arrangement makes it clear that we are dealing with a poem. On the other hand, where rhymed prose was involved, either in the primary documents or in Spiegel's discussion, I have retained the rhyme effects in order not to obliterate the special character of the sentences. Since Rabbi Ephraim's poem is here translated for the first time, I felt that it would be of greater service to readers and students to render it as literally as possible.

In the notes I have *not* retained Spiegel's style. Here too there are a number of graceful allusions and echoes, for example, "and above all 'beware lest you overlook that one called Levi,' Professor Louis Ginzberg, *Commentary on the Palestinian Talmud,* III, pp. 238 et seq." (see Deut. 12:19); or, "my master and teacher R. Avigdor (Viktor) Aptowitzer." All such expressions have been stripped to the barest statement, for while in Hebrew such courtliness not only has its place but reflects the elegant pirouette, the reverence toward great scholars and scholarship, in the usage of modern English footnotes they are comic and incongruous.

[22] Cf. Ginzberg, *Legends,* I, 217; V, 218, n. 52.

In citing Bible verses and passages I have chosen no version con-
sistently. What the context demanded, be it Midrash or Piyyut or
author's argument, determined the rendition of the verse. That is
why even the same verse will not necessarily appear the same way
all the time. Perhaps this itself may remind the reader how plastic
the Scriptural vocabulary remained in the hands of all who loved
the words of the Law and the prophets. I should say, however, that
I found the new version of the Pentateuch prepared under the aus-
pices of the Jewish Publication Society of America particularly use-
ful and rewarding.

For the first 15 pages of the present volume, I drew on a draft
by Jacob Sloan, to whom I wish to express my thanks. In preparing
the literal rendering of Rabbi Ephraim's poem and the poetry quoted
in the course of discussion, I had Grace Goldin's open-handed assis-
tance. Robin Goldin helped in the preparation of the typescript.
Professor Spiegel granted me many hours for consultation on translation problems. And I am grateful to the American Council of
Learned Societies for encouraging me to put *Me-Aggadot ha-Akedah* into English.

IX

Me-Aggadot ha-Akedah, as I said at the outset, was originally published in the Jubilee Volume honoring the late Alexander Marx.
Obviously, this study is Spiegel's to dedicate. But since almost all
the time I worked on the translation another person kept coming
to my mind, I hope it is no infringement to dedicate *The Last Trial*
to the noble memory of Röslein Spiegel.

J.G.

Davenport College
Yale University
December 1966

THE LAST TRIAL

PROLOGUE

Even the ancients, long ago, were surprised that immediately after the Akedah—after Isaac was bound on the altar to be sacrificed by his father at God's command, and then just as categorically ordered to be released and not to be even so much as bruised—that immediately after that, all traces of Isaac son of Father Abraham disappear. In the account of the journey *to* Mount Moriah, both father and son are mentioned by Scripture, "And they went both of them together" (Gen. 22:6-8), the one to make the offering and the other to be the offering; but in connection with the descent from the mountain, it does not say, "So *they* returned to the young men," but "So *Abraham returned* [in the singular!] to the young men" (v. 19). One would think it was only the father who returned, and his son was not with him.

Where was Isaac?

To this question we already have answers from the second generation of Palestinian Amoraim, from the disciples and colleagues of Rabbi Johanan. "And Isaac, where was he?" R. Yose bar Haninah replied: When Isaac's father perceived that a miracle had occurred, "he sent him home in the night, lest the Evil Eye affect him." [1] According to R. Eleazar ben Pedat, "Although Isaac did not die, Scrip-

---

[1] Genesis Rabba 56, end. Yalkut, #102.

ture regards him *as though* he had died and his ashes lay piled on the altar. That is why it is said, 'So Abraham returned unto his young men.' " [2]

Still another view of the matter among the Babylonian sages: R. Berekiah reported in the name of the "masters there" that (immediately after the Akedah) Isaac's father "had sent him off to study Torah with Shem. It's to be compared to a woman who grows rich from plying her distaff. She says to herself: 'Since this distaff has made me rich, it will never leave my hand.' In the same way Abraham said to himself: 'Everything I gained I have gained only because I engaged in the study of Torah and in carrying out God's commandments. That is why I do not want such practice ever to leave my seed.' Thereafter Isaac passed three years in the Great Study House of Shem and Eber." [3]

The masters of Midrash furnished their interpretations; and then along came the exegetes with their comments: because they found additional things to wonder about. When Abraham came to mourn for Sarah and to bewail her, why did not Isaac come along? [4] What is more, not a word about him even in the account of the mission of Eliezer (Gen. 24), until Eliezer returned with Rebeccah! [5]

---

[2] Midrash ha-Gadol *ad* Gen. 22:19, ed. M. Margulies (Jerusalem, 1947), p. 360 [hereafter abbr. MhG].

[3] Gen. R., loc. cit. Targum Jonathan, Gen. 22:19: "And the angels on high led Isaac and brought him to the Great Study House of Shem; and there he remained three years." See also the Midrash quoted in Yalkut, #98, and this source is the Midrash Composed under the Holy Spirit, published by Jacob Mann in *The Bible as Read and Preached in the Old Synagogue* (Cincinnati, 1940), pp. 65ff. [hereafter abbr. Mann]. This is the source for MhG, Gen. 22:8: "Is this the *great*

[*house of*] *study* you told my brother of?" Cf. ibid., 22:19: "He went to Shem ben Noah to study." In Midrash Aggadah, ed. S. Buber: "Where is Isaac? He replied, I brought him to the house of his teacher Eber, to study Torah." In Sefer ha-Yashar, ed. Eliezer Goldschmidt (Berlin, 1923), p. 75: "I shall bring him to Shem and his son Eber"; p. 82: "the house of Shem and Eber." As for the Age of Shem and Eber, cf. Seder Olam, ed. Alexander Marx (Berlin, 1903), end of ch. 1 and beginning of ch. 2, and notes ibid.

[4] Cf. R. Bahya *ad* Gen. 23:2.

[5] Joseph ibn Kaspi, Mishneh Kesef on the

The grammarians, of course, were ready with their solutions: Only Abraham is mentioned because, although there were others like Isaac in the mourning company, Abraham was the central and principal figure. "In the Torah there are hundreds and thousands of such" grammatical constructions.[6] Somewhat similar is the commentary of Abraham ibn Ezra:[7] It stands to reason that Isaac is not mentioned, because he was still under thirteen years of age and hence under the jurisdiction of his father. Others speculated that perhaps Isaac had remained "on Mount Moriah for three years until he reached the age of forty, and then he married Rebeccah."[8] Or: "Perhaps on the return from Moriah, as Isaac came along to hear what his father would tell the young men of what had taken place—or perhaps Abraham would keep altogether quiet about the whole incident—Isaac rather lagged in his petty pace, possibly because of the shock from having been tied up and bound; out of weariness, he fell behind in his walking."[9] Or perhaps Isaac's father had sent him "home to Hebron by another route to bring the glad tidings to Sarah and relieve her of her sorrow."[10] There is no lack of other solutions, all of a similar flavor.

And then there are those who took off to the outer space of the miraculous for their solutions: "And Isaac, where was he? The Holy One, blessed be He, brought him into the Garden of Eden, and there he stayed three years."[11]

Pentateuch, ed. Isaac ha-Levi Last (Cracow, 1906), II, p. 63.

[6] Cf. Kimhi's Pentateuch Commentary, ed. Abraham Ginzburg (Pressburg, 1842), 55b, and Ibn Kaspi, op. cit., whose words I quoted in the text; cf. also N. H. Wessely, *Imre Shefer* (Lyck, 1869), 220a.

[7] *Ad* Gen. 22:5, 19.

[8] R. Bahya, loc. cit.

[9] Midrashe ha-Torah, by En Saloma Astruc, ed. Simeon Eppenstein (Berlin, 1899), p. 36.

[10] Abrabanel *ad* Gen. 22:19.

[11] MhG on 22:19. And so, too, the poet Benjamin bar Samuel of Coutances speaks of Isaac spending three years in Paradise, in a Kerobah for the Feast of Shabuot,

Then on occasion the Akedah theme was tied into one knot with
the legend of the virtues of Eliezer, Abraham's senior servant, who
carried out his mission faithfully but had been suspected gratu-
itously—and for that reason was found worthy of being included
in the number of those righteous men who never knew the taste
of death; for the ministering angels had led him up into Paradise
during his lifetime: "Here is a wonder indeed! Isaac *emerged* from
Paradise alive, while Eliezer *entered* Paradise alive." [12] The hint for
that is, of course, in Scripture (Gen. 24:62, 63) : "And Isaac came
from the way of Beer-le-hai-roi . . . And Isaac went out . . ."
Whence did he go out? From Paradise. [13] No wonder Rebeccah lost
her equilibrium "and she fell from the camel" (v. 64)—for what
she perceived was Isaac coming down from Paradise, and he walked
the way the dead walk, head down and feet up. [14] And what was he
doing all that time in Paradise? "They were healing him there." [15]
When was that? After the incident on Mount Moriah: "And the
angels bore him to Paradise, where he tarried three years, to be
healed from the wound inflicted upon him by Abraham on the occasion of the Akedah." [16]

Isaac ben Asher ha-Levi, one of the first Tosafists in medieval
Germany, or Ashkenaz, [17] "found a midrash in which is said that

"Longer than the earth, wider than the
sea." See L. Zunz, *Literaturgeschichte
der synagogalen Poesie* (Berlin, 1865),
p. 291 [hereafter abbr. *Literaturgeschichte*]. The Kerobah has disappeared
and was not copied from the Turin Mahzor; cf. I. Davidson, Seder Hibbur Berakot, *JQR*, XXI (1931), 252.

[12] Yalkut, #109. Cf. Michael Higger,
Massektot Zeirot, pp. 74 and 130, and
Massektot Derek Eres, p. 68. See Louis
Ginzberg, *Legends of the Jews* (Phila-
delphia, 1909ff.), V, p. 96 [hereafter
abbr. *Legends*].

[13] Hadar Zekenim, Baale ha-Tosafot al
ha-Torah (Leghorn, 1840), 9b.

[14] Minhat Yehudah, by R. Judah bar
Eliezer (printed together with Daat
Zekenim) *ad* Gen. 24:64, and Paaneah
Raza, by R. Isaac bar Juda ha-Levi
(Tarnopol, 1813), 29a.

[15] Paaneah Raza, loc. cit.

[16] Yalkut Reubeni, Wa-Yera (Maggid,
Toledot).

[17] His dates are approximately 1050-1130.
See the introduction to Sefer Rabiah, ed.
V. Aptowitzer, p. 369.

Isaac was secreted in Paradise for two years in order to be healed from the incision made in him by his father when he began to offer him up as a sacrifice." [18]

This legend travelled far during the Middle Ages; we find its traces in Spain in the time of Joseph ibn Kaspi.[19] "When I was in the city of Valencia some years back, the Lord in His goodness allowed me to run into a saintly and distinguished elder, who had [20] a long beard, all white; he told me the reason Isaac did not return (from Moriah with his father) was that the Lord had sent him to Paradise, as a reward for all he had suffered when about to be slain. There he remained until he was to marry the lovely Rebeccah. That is why there is no mention of Isaac's name, neither in the account of Sarah's death nor of Eliezer's mission. . . . I said to him: 'Your heart be blessed for putting my mind to rest.' "

Support for this legend was found in the Song of Songs, as R. Joshua ibn Shuaib[21] of that generation testifies: "In the opinion of the Midrash, he [Isaac] was not in that city [Hebron] at the time, because he was in Paradise, to recover from the effects on his neck of what his father did to him during the Akedah, which left a mark in the shape of a bead. And that is why it is written (Cant. 4:9), 'With one bead of thy necklace.' In Paradise he tarried three years, as it is written (Gen. 24:62), *bo mi-bo* (come from the way, come from *bo'*), the numerical value of the consonants *b* and '*o* (of the word *bo'*) equals three."

---

[18] Hadar Zekenim 10b (= *Bet ha-Mid-rash*, ed. Jellinek, V. p. 157) and Minhat Yehudah, Toledot, Gen. 25:27; cf. Hizkuni *ad* Gen. 22:19.

[19] Mishneh Kesef on Pentateuch, p. 63. Ibn Kaspi from the city of L'Argentière (Hebrew: ksp̄, silver), in Languedoc, visited Valencia in Spain in the month of Elul of 1332, as can be seen from his

Sefer ha-Musar sent from there to his son in Tarascon; cf. Israel Abrahams, *Hebrew Ethical Wills* (Philadelphia, 1926), pp. 131 and 161.

[20] Printed version, '*m* (with); read: *lo* (he had).

[21] Sefer Derashot (Cracow, 1573), Hayye Sarah, 96.

In the course of his wanderings Abraham ibn Ezra[22] also picked
up a similar legend. " 'And Abraham returned'—and Isaac is not
mentioned. . . . But he who asserts that *Abraham slew Isaac and
abandoned him, and that afterwards Isaac came to life again*, is
speaking contrary to Writ." Apparently Ibn Ezra wants to say that
by the words (Gen. 22:12) "Lay not thy hand upon the lad, neither
do thou anything (*meumah*) unto him," the Torah is underscoring
what the talmudic Sages teach, "Don't you even so much as *bruise
(mumah)* him." [23] It is as though the literal meaning of Scripture
forbids and makes impossible this strange legend—which is in fact
a flat denial of the biblical account.

Any deviation from the patent sense of Scripture calls for an
explanation—always, let alone in the Middle Ages. In a milieu so
totally committed to the inherited, clinging to the old and habitually
devoted to its traditions, how could there have arisen, and then even
have been disseminated, such paradoxical haggadic lore? What
compelled the faithful of Israel to depart from the clear statement
of Scripture and from what was public knowledge among this people and every other people? The story of the Akedah—is it possible
that these pious generations failed to be affected by the plain meaning of the words of Scripture?

[22] In his commentary *ad* Gen. 22:19.   [23] Gen. R. 56:7; cf. Rashi *ad* Gen. 22:12.

I

*But quarrelsome critics who misconstrue everything . . .
do not think Abraham's action great or wonderful.*[1]

There survives in the writings of Philo an echo of the kind of
criticism that could be overheard in his day of the story of Father
Abraham. To be sure, the Alexandrian thinker could sweep away
criticism and critics alike, and upbraid them as captious and hostile;
they prefer slander to giving credit where credit is due, and delight
in minimizing or destroying examples of noble conduct, out of spite
or downright hatred of excellence.[2] It is out of odiousness that they
are fond of citing again and again examples of other fathers who
had sacrificed sons or daughters whom they loved, for the good of
their nation, or to appease the gods, or in times of wars, of droughts
and flood and pestilences, to make atonement for their countries.[3]
According to these critics, there is nothing extraordinary to Abraham's conduct, and his readiness to offer up Isaac is in no way
superior to the heroic acts and self-sacrifice among many noble
pagans, who, put to similar tests—and some even more demanding
than these—endured them readily in times of crisis.

In antiquity, a reader was sure to be familiar with stories of this
kind about renowned heroes in history; there was no need for Philo

---

[1] Philo, *De Abrahamo* 33.178.
[2] Ibid. 191, 199.

[3] Ibid. 178: λυτήρια ἢ πολέμων ἢ αὐχμῶν ἢ
ἐπομβρίας ἢ νοσημάτων.

to list their names or their acts in detail. In Athens, near the Boule, stood statues of the city's founding fathers, the heads of the ten original tribes. In their midst rose the statue of Leos, son of Orpheus. Of him it was told that there was a famine in his days; and, the oracle at Delphi having been consulted and having answered that the gods would certainly relent towards the country if human sacrifice were offered up, he took his three daughters and sacrificed them to bring salvation to his people.[4] Whereupon the famine was checked in Athens. According to another version, the girls volunteered for the sacrifice,[5] father and daughters going together,[6] of one mind and single-minded, the father rejoicing to slay, the daughters rejoicing to be slain. Indeed, the maids of Leos[7] became in time a model and example of love for the fatherland.

Other Greek tribes had similar traditions. In the region of Messenia, Aristodemus was celebrated as a man without fear, as a champion of his people. In his days a plague broke out; it fell to the lot of the daughter of Lyciscus to be sacrificed on the altar. Father and daughter fled to Sparta. Then Aristodemus went down to the gate of the city and there of his own free will offered up his own daughter to the gods and wrought salvation for all.[8] Who of the Greeks had not heard of the fame and praises of Agamemnon, who did not forbear to sacrifice his daughter Iphigenia? Happily the goddess Artemis took pity and substituted a hind for the girl, and the girl she carried off in a cloud to become a priestess in her sanctuary.[9]

---

[4] Pausanias, *Graeciae Descriptio* 1.5.2: Λεώς· δοῦναι δὲ ἐπὶ σωτηρίᾳ κοινῇ λέγεται τὰς θυγατέρας τοῦ θεοῦ χρήσαντος.

[5] Jerome, *Adversus Jovinianum* 1.41 (Migne, *P. L.* xxiii, col. 270): "spontanea morte."

[6] Philo, op. cit., 172: "Together" (Gen. 22:6, 8), "They walked with equal speed

of mind rather than body"; cf. idem, *De migratione Abrahami*, 166 sq.

[7] Λεὼ κόραι: Diodorus Siculus, *Bibliotheca historica* 17.15.

[8] Pausanias, 4.9.4 sq.

[9] *Cypria*, ed. Kinkel, p. 19; Aeschylus, *Agamemnon* 1534; Euripides, *Iphigenia*

Then there was the tale of the miracle of Phrixus, first born of the royal house of Athamas, son of Aeolus. His people wished to sacrifice Phrixus in a year of drought; but the god sent a ram that delivered him and carried him off from the place of sacrifice. And after he was rescued, Phrixus took the ram and sacrificed it as a thanksgiving offering to his god who had delivered him.[10]

The Greeks were acquainted with similar miracles that were to be found not merely in legends. There was the famous story of Pelopidas, to whom a god appeared one night in a dream[11] promising him victory if Pelopidas would offer up a virgin with auburn hair as a sacrifice. As the commanding general hesitated, wavering and being of two minds about it, behold, a mare broke from the pasturing herd and headed in leaps and bounds straight for his tent. And while everyone was still gaping at the beauty of its fiery mane, the seer Theocritus addressed Pelopidas as follows: "Here is your victim, O warrior! From heaven a virgin with auburn hair has been appointed for you." [12] The mare was sacrificed forthwith and Pelopidas's forces struck their enemy a fatal blow; for it pleased the gods to accept an animal sacrifice in lieu of a human sacrifice.

The fact is, the world both of myth and of reality furnished the Greeks with legends and traditions along the lines of the Mount Moriah story, and it is hardly surprising that some should conclude that in their own wonderful stories there were mightily greater elements than in that which told of what happened to Abraham. Philo

---

at *Aulis* 1540, *Jphigenia in Tauris* 20.30.-783; Ovid, *Metamorphoses* 12.245 sqq. Cf. Lucretius, *De rerum natura* 1.101: "Tantum religio potuit suadere malorum!" See above, n. 1.

[10] Apollodorus, *Bibliotheca* 1.9.1 sq.; Herodotus 7.197; Plutarch, *De superstitione* 5.

[11] Cf. D. Kimhi: " 'And He said to him, Abraham' (Gen. 22:1), *in a night vision* He spoke to him, for note, it goes on to say, 'So Abraham rose early in the morning' " (v. 3).

[12] Plutarch, *Vitae parallelae*, Pelopidas c. 21. See Joshua Finkel, "Old Israelitish Tradition in the Koran," *Proceedings of the American Academy for Jewish Research*, 1931, p. 15.

goes to great pains to remove from the minds of his readers the notion that there was any comparison between what occurred at the Akedah and human sacrifice among the pagans. At great length he insists that Abraham did what he did not out of conformity to ancestral practice, or under some pressure to relieve public distress, or out of a running after glory—why, at the time of the Akedah there wasn't a soul with him, to be able subsequently to broadcast his piety![13] No, Abraham served his Creator out of love, with his whole heart, not with part of it—not as though in part his heart went out to Isaac and in part yielded only out of fear of Heaven.[14] And because he gave everything to his God in obedience to His sacred word, the Lord returned that gift to him and reckoned it to his merit. True enough, the act was *not entirely consummated,* nevertheless, the consummation to be wished was genuinely there,[15] and the record is engraved on the tables of the Holy Books and on the tables of the hearts of all who meditate thereon.

[13] Cf. D. Kimhi: "There was no one there . . . only Abraham and his son Isaac. . . . Who then could have publicized this thing in the world? And even if he had himself told of it, who would have believed him?" In Philo's words you will find something of the distinctions drawn by S. Kierkegaard in *Fear and Trembling* (Copenhagen, 1843): the difference between a "tragic hero" like Agamemnon and "the knight of faith" like Abraham.

[14] *De Abrahamo* 198.

[15] Ibid. 177: ἡ πρᾶξις, εἰ καὶ μὴ τὸ τέλος ἐπηκολούθησεν, ὁλόκληρος καὶ παντελὴς οὐ μόνον ἐν ταῖς ἱεραῖς βίβλοις ἀλλὰ καὶ ἐν ταῖς τῶν ἀναγινωσκόντων διανοίαις ἀνάγραπτος ἐστηλίτευται.

II

*Abraham, don't let your thoughts grow proud!
You brought one offering on one altar, and I on
seven altars offered sacrifices!* [1]

Jason of Cyrene, the historian of the first generation of the Has-
monean dynasty, included in his book a description of the heroes
of the faith who during the persecutions of Antiochus IV sanctified
God's Name by martyrdom. All that has remained of Jason's work
is a summary or abridgment [2] drawn up by the author of II Maccabees, in the Apocrypha. And perhaps all the other books about the
Hasmoneans also survived only by virtue of their accounts of the
trials and torments suffered by the martyrs, [3] for in them the Christian Church discovered prototypes of the witnesses for the faith,
or of martyrs who are persecuted and slain for the sake of their
religion. [4] In Jewish literature, of all the stories told either by Jason
or his epitomizer, the favorite has become that of The Woman and
Her Seven Sons, [5] who refused to bow down to the idol, and every

---

[1] Yalkut, Lamentations, #1029.

[2] ἐπιτομή; cf. II Maccabees 2:23-28.

[3] Chs. 6 and 7 of II Mac. were expanded
in IV Mac.: the story about Eleazar
(5:4ff.) and the story of the mother and
the seven brothers (8:3ff.).

[4] Augustine, *De civitate Dei* 18.36. Cf.
Elias J. Bickerman, *Der Gott der Makka-*

bäer (Berlin, 1937), p. 36; idem, in *Louis
Ginzberg Jubilee Volume* (New York,
1945), pp. 106ff.

[5] B. Gittin 57b (woman and her seven
sons) and so too Yalkut, Lam., #1029;
Seder Eliyahu Rabba, ch. 28 (widow and
her seven sons), cf. M. Friedmann, p.
151, n. 17. Lam. R. 1 (the story of

one of them died for the Sanctification of the Name. Legend exalted and embroidered the details of their heroism and their skill at retorting to their enemies and tempters. Both the mother and her sons were endowed with the grace and strength of an unblemished faith. And thus, in the course of time, they were transformed into a noble paradigm of loving acceptance of suffering for the sake of the Unification of the Name.

What is more, before long the specifically historical features of the story were blurred in the folk memory, and anachronistically the legend was transferred to the period of the Hadrianic persecutions, when the Roman emperor undertook once for all an extirpation of the Jews and Jewish teaching.[6] Now to the story of the widow and her seven sons was added the new dimension of flaming zeal in that desperate war against Rome, the pride of the holy stiff-neckedness of those murdered by the Empire, those who put up their whole life in behalf of the Redeemer of Israel. The temper of these generations found expression in the symbol of this *mater dolorosa* who sacrificed all her sons for love of the Torah and fear of God. Into her mouth the haggadah of the talmudic Rabbis put words which expressed the mood of innumerable fathers and moth-

---

Miriam, daughter of Nahtom), ed. Buber, p. 84 (daughter of Tanhum). Pesikta Rabbati, ch. 43, 180b (Miriam, daughter of Tanhum), and so too Yalkut *ad Deut.* 26, #938. Josippon, ch. 19 (seven brothers, sons of the same mother, and the mother's name was *Hannah*). Cf. Midrash on the Ten Commandments (*Bet ha-Midrash*, ed. Jellinek, I, p. 70) and S. Loewinger in *Tiferet Hayyim,* jubilee vol. in honor of Rabbi Hayyim Zevi Kisch (Budapest, 1939), p. 41—a Budapest MS account which ties together the story of the mother and her seven sons with the haggadah about the Ten Slain by the

Roman Empire. [Cf. Gerson D. Cohen, "The Story of Hannah and Her Seven Sons in Hebrew Literature," in *Mordecai M. Kaplan Jubilee Volume* (New York, 1953), Hebrew sec. pp. 109ff.]

[6] Seder Eliyahu Rabba, ch. 28: "Emperor Hadrian." Pesikta R., ch. 43: "In the days of the *Shemad.*" On the persecutions in the days of the Emperor Hadrian, see Saul Lieberman, "The Martyrs of Caesarea," in *Annuaire de l'Université Libre de Bruxelles, Inst. de philol. et d'hist. orient. et slaves,* VII (New York, 1944), pp. 427ff.

ers during the *Shemad* period, the period of the Hadrianic devastations—parents who both mourned and rejoiced, mourning on the one hand because it had been decreed that their sons must be slain, rejoicing on the other hand because through their sons Heaven's glory was sanctified: "Their mother wept and said to them: Children, do not be distressed, for to this end were you created—to sanctify in the world the Name of the Holy One, blessed be He. Go and tell Father Abraham: Let not your heart swell with pride! You built one altar, but I have built seven altars and on them have offered up my seven sons. What is more: Yours was a trial; mine was an accomplished fact!" [7]

In the light of the historical reality of the second-century persecutions under the Roman Empire, it seemed almost as though something of the splendor and awe of the biblical Akedah story was diminished. Who cares about some ancient, far off in time, who was merely *thought of as a possible* sacrifice on the altar, but who was delivered from the danger, whom no misfortune overtook; when right before your eyes, in the immediate present, fathers and sons *en masse* ascend the executioner's block to be butchered and burned, literally butchered and burned?

Your nearest of kin is you, and the sheer number of victims is enough to terrify you. But even more maddening is the gulf between intention and act. How compare one who puts his son on top of the altar and then takes him down again sound of limb with one who offers up his son and never takes him down, or if he does, does it only to put him deep into the pit? Is one who plans an act but does not act it out like the one who actually did act it out? For the former there is still a future, still hope for reward; but the latter is

---

[7] Yalkut, Deut. 26, #938; and cf. Lam. R., p. 85: "You built one altar *and did not offer up your son*, but I built seven altars and offered up my sons on them," etc.

heir only to frightful torments and an ugly death! More of life and
its gifts are reserved for the former; the latter's cup is brimful of
grief and the grave. *Then,* in the Torah: And the Lord changed the
fortune of Abraham, and Isaac survived intact and tranquil. *But
now,* in the actualities of the murders perpetrated by the Roman
Empire: Men give one final gasp, and there's an end! Earth stops
the victim's mouth. Worlds separate the *readiness* to submit to the
will of Heaven from the *actual* Sanctification of Heaven's Name.
Here is the boundary between the quick and the dead! And through
the outcry of that mother in the talmudic haggadah, the whole
Shemad generation registered its pain and the formidable achieve-
ments of its children that could make the biblical hero blush: Yours
was a *trial,* mine were the *performances!*[8]

[8] Lam. R., loc. cit.; cf. *Tiferet Hayyim,*
p. 42: "Go and tell Father Abraham *not
to puff up his heart;* if he made an
Akedah of one son, I made an Akedah
of seven."

III

*Can you even count the number of those transfixed
In the years 1096 and 1146?*[1]

"In trying to tell of the wrath and the rage, not a heart has the
strength, the hand fails on the page":[2] in such or similar terms the
chroniclers of the nightmare period of the Crusades apologize and
then attempt to go on with their accounts. They registered each of
the disasters studiously, for the memory of every disastrous event
and their deliverance therefrom was precious to them; and although
it was beyond their powers, they labored to put down on paper
every decree and every persecution of their times—first as a record
for posterity, and second (indeed, this seemed their primary mo-
tive) to strengthen failing hearts here and now. It is apparent from
the language of these records that they were written in the first place
for synagogue purposes, as reading matter along with public recitation of prayers, as liturgical poetry and penitential hymns based on
current events.[3]

---

[1] R. Eliezer bar Nathan in his Selihah
(penitential poem) "The Covenant and
the Oath"; cf. A. M. Habermann, *Sefer
Gezerot Ashkenaz we-Sarefat* (Jerusalem,
1945), p. 108 [hereafter abbr. Haber-
mann].

[2] A. Neubauer and M. Stern, *Hebräische*

*Berichte über die Judenverfolgungen
während der Kreuzzüge* (Berlin, 1892), p.
31 [hereafter abbr. NS] = Habermann,
p. 142.

[3] See, for example, Sefer Zekirah by R.
Ephraim of Bonn (NS, p. 69 = Habermann, p. 126, and notes p. 257): "And

In the Synagogue on the eve of Rosh ha-Shanah one still reads
a penitential prayer,[4] its language reminiscent of the Chronicle of
1096, about the martyrs of Magenza (Mainz), *magen we-zinah,*
"Shield and Buckler of every congregation."[5] At first the Jews of
that city tried to take refuge behind the fortified courtyard of the
archbishop and to defend themselves. "Young and old donned
armor and with weapons girded themselves, and with R. Kalonymos
the Parnas in the lead . . . they made their way to the gate to
battle against the vagabonds and the townspeople. . . . But oh, because of our sins the enemy prevailed and captured the gateway."[6]
And when the Jews discovered that the mobsters had broken
through into the castle courtyard and there was no way out except
through apostasy, they resolved to delay no further: "Their voice
rang out because all hearts were at one: 'Hear, O Israel, the Lord
. . . is One.' Ours not to question the ways of the Holy One,
blessed be He and blessed be His Name, for it is He who gave us
His Torah, He who commanded that we die and be slain for the
Unification of His Holy Name. . . . Oh, our good fortune if we
do His will! Oh, the good fortune of everyone slain and butchered
and killed for the *Unification of His Name.* There is *none better*
to sacrifice our lives to *than our God.*[7] Let every one who has a
knife inspect it lest it be flawed. Let him come forth and cut our

---

above it is written in the Selihot on the
calamity at Blois." So, then, the events
were recorded in his commentary on the
Mahzor. See Zunz, *Ritus* (Berlin, 1859),
p. 196, and M. Steinschneider, *Catalog
der Handschriften in der Stadtbibliothek
zu Hamburg* (Hamburg, 1878), p. 57.

[4] It begins: "Oh do take a look at the
righteousness of Thy servants, Thy
saints"; cf. Israel Davidson, *Thesaurus
of Medieval Hebrew Poetry* (New York,
1924-33), I, p. 286, #6274 [hereafter

abbr. Davidson].

[5] NS, p. 2 = Habermann, p. 26.

[6] NS, pp. 6, 53 = Habermann, pp. 30, 99f.

[7] NS, p. 7 = p. 53 = Habermann, p.
31 = p. 100. Cf. Yizhak Baer in the
introduction to *Sefer Gezerot Ashkenaz
we-Sarefat* (Habermann, p. 4), on the
influence of the Hebrew Josippon on the
storytellers and the very protagonists.
See in Josippon, ch. 92, the reply of
Yohanan, "the leader of the rebels," to

throats for the sanctification of Him who Alone lives Eternally; and
finally let him cut his own throat. . . . Whereupon all of them,
men and women, rose and slew each other. . . . The tender of
heart put on courage and themselves cut the throats of their wives
and children, yea, babes. The tenderest and the daintiest of women
cut the throat of her darling child. . . . Women bared their necks
to one another in order to be offered up for the Unification of the
Name. So a man treated his own son and his own brother; so a
brother his own sister; so a woman her own son and daughter; so
a man his neighbor and comrade, bridegroom his bride, lover his
beloved—here is one sacrificing and then himself being sacrificed,
and there another sacrificing and himself being sacrificed—until
there was one flood of blood, the blood of husbands running together with that of their wives, the blood of fathers with that of
their children, the blood of brothers with that of their sisters, the
blood of masters with that of their disciples, the blood of bridegrooms with that of their brides, the blood of those who chant the
liturgy with that of those who compose the sacred songs, the blood
of babes and sucklings with that of their mothers; and so they were
slain and sacrificed for the Unification of the Glorious and Awesome Name.[8] . . . Ask ye now and see, was there ever such a

Titus: "There is no better sacrifice to
our Lord in the Temple than our own
flesh, and there is nothing better to spray
in His Sanctuary and Temple than our
own blood. For our God we shall die,
we shall make battle, and may we be
regarded before Him as His acceptable
burnt-offerings and lambs, and we shall
die free men inside the Holy City and
not as slaves at your hands." See also
ibid., ch. 71: "Let us die for His covenant,
for His Torah, for His Sanctuary along
with His servants who are slain for the
Unity of His Great Name." This idiom
occurs frequently in the records from the
days of the Crusaders. Cf. Lekah Tob,
end of Niṣabim (Deut. 30): " 'And to
cleave unto Him' refers to the unifying
of His Name." As for the mention of the
Akedah in Josippon: ch. 97 derives apparently from Christian sources; cf. Hebrews 11:17-19.

[8] So, too, in the Selihah mentioned above,
"Oh do take a look": the blood of fathers
and sons came together, the blood of
compassionate women and that of their
children; mixed was the blood of brothers and sisters, the blood of bridegrooms
and brides, etc.

holocaust as this since the days of Adam? When were there ever
a thousand and a hundred sacrifices in one day, *each and every one
of them like the Akedah of Isaac son of Abraham?* Once at the
Akedah of one on Mount Moriah, the Lord shook the world to its
base! . . . O heavens, why did you not go black, O stars, why did
you not withdraw your light, O sun and moon, why did you not
darken in your sky? °—when in one day one thousand and one
hundred pure souls were slain and slaughtered! Oh the spotless
babes and sucklings, innocent of all sin, oh the innocent lives! Wilt
Thou hold Thy peace in the face of these things, O Lord?" [10]

Questions like these, raging laments from hearts in a whirlpool of
torment, recur in the synagogue poetry of that generation, ringing
every note on the scale of grief and shock:

O Lord, Mighty One, dwelling on high!
Once, over one Akedah, Ariels cried out before Thee.
But now how many are butchered and burned!
Why over the blood of children did they not raise a cry? [11]

Before that patriarch could in his haste sacrifice his only one,
It was heard from heaven: Do not put forth your hand to destroy!
But now how many sons and daughters of Judah are slain—

---

[9] Based on the biblical expression, Isa.
5:30; cf. Rashi *ad loc.*: "Some interpret
the word ṣar as a reference to the moon,
the smaller constellation, and 'or as a
reference to the sun." D. Kimhi: "And
some explain ṣar and 'or as sun and
moon. The heavens are called 'arifim
because they drop rain, as it is said
(Deut. 33:28), 'Under heavens dripping
(ya 'arfu) dew.' "

[10] NS, pp. 8, 39, 53 = Habermann, pp.
32, 75, 100. And so too in the Selihah
"Oh do take a look": Remember these
altars. Regard these Akedot. For over

one He stormed the world. And behold,
Ariels in outer space screamed. All the
more now, *numbers upon numbers of
Akedot*, they sacrificed their sons for
the *Unity of Thy Name* which is Glorious
(Selihot, ed. W. Heidenheim, Roedelheim,
1833, #57, 77b).

[11] Selihah: "I shall speak in the grief of
my spirit." It may be that in the first
stanza the author may have put his name
by acrostic signature: Abraham. Cf.
Hayyim Schirmann, *Kobeṣ al Yad*, N.S.,
III (Jerusalem, 1939), p. 31, and Habermann, p. 62.

While yet He makes no haste to save those butchered nor those
cast on the flames.[12]

On the merit of the Akedah at Moriah once we could lean,
Safeguarded for the salvation of age after age—
Now one Akedah follows another, they cannot be counted.[13]

No, the memory of Mount Moriah had not faded; it continued
to instruct every one who followed the course of Sanctification of
the Name. But for the victims of the Crusades it was impossible not
to feel that their sufferings and sacrifices exceeded by far everything
endured by the original Akedah father and son. So the synagogue
poets, the *payyetanim*, go on singing the praises of their contemporary fathers and sons, who enacted to the last line everything
reported in rabbinic sources of Abraham and Isaac, and surpassed
that:

How the outcry of the children rises!
Trembling, they see their brothers slain.
The mother binds her son lest he be blemished as he startles,
The father makes a blessing before slaughtering the sacrifice.[14]

To their mothers in grief the tender children say,
Offer us up as a whole burnt offering! We are wanted on high! . . .
With their fathers the sturdy young men plead,

[12] Fragment from a Threnody by R. Eliezer
bar Joel ha-Levi; cf. Zunz, *Literatur-*
geschichte, p. 327, n. 1, and Davidson,
Thesaurus, II, p. 161, #1041. The poem
was published in S. Bernfeld, *Sefer ha-*
Demaot, I, p. 209, and in intro. to Sefer
Rabiah, p. 139.

[13] "O God, do not hush up the shedding
of my blood!" by R. David bar Meshullam, Selihot, ed. Heidenheim, Roedelheim,
#49, 66b; Hayyim Brody, *Mibhar ha-*
Shirah ha-Ivrit, p. 223; *Sefer ha-Demaot*,
I, p. 202; Habermann, p. 71.

[14] Schirmann, p. 30; cf. above, n. 11. See
Targum Jonathan and Targum Jerushalmi
ad Gen. 22:9: "Bind me properly lest
I start *suddenly*, and there (will) occur
a blemish in your offering." See, below,
the *Akedah* of R. Ephraim of Bonn, line
41, and nn.

Quick! Hurry to do our Creator's will! . . .
His father tied him who was offered on Mount Moriah,
Who prayed he should not kick and disqualify the slaughter.
But we without being tied are slain for His love . . .[15]

What such verses mean is made fully clear by the Chronicles of
the times. For example, it is reported of the martyrs of Weve-
linghofen: "Men, women, and children, bridegrooms and brides,
old men and old women, for the sanctification of the One Name,
killed themselves—offered their throats to be cut, their heads to be
severed, in the ditches of water surrounding the town."[16] Now there
was a certain saintly man there, an elder well on in years, and his name
was Rabbenu Samuel bar Yehiel. He had an only son, a splendid
looking young man, who with his father fled into the water and there
offered his throat for slaughter by his father. Whereupon the father
recited the appropriate blessing for the slaughter of cattle and fowl,
and the son responded with 'Amen.' And all those who were standing around them responded in a loud voice, 'Hear, O Israel, the
Lord our God, the Lord is One.' O citizens of the world, take a
good look! How extraordinary was the stamina of the son who
unbound let himself be slaughtered, and how extraordinary was
the stamina of the father who could resist compassion for an *only*
son, so splendid and handsome a young man. Can anyone hear of
this and remain dry-eyed?—the sacrifice and the sacrificer of one
mind and in one assent to death. Oh, it is of them and the likes of
them that it is said (Ps. 50:23), 'It is the one who offers a sacrifice
of thanksgiving who honors Me.'[17] Now it came to pass that when

---

[15] Selihah by R. Eliezer bar Nathan: "O
God, vandals have risen against us." Cf.
Zevi Lichtenstein, *Zeitschrift für die
Geschichte der Juden in Deutschland,* II
(1930), 238, and Habermann, p. 86.
[16] Ditches of water: "der mit Wasser

gefüllte Burggraben"; cf. Siegmund Salfeld, *Das Martyrologium des Nürnberger
Memorbuches* (Berlin, 1898), p. 420
[hereafter abbr. Salfeld].
[17] NS, p. 41 = Habermann, p. 77.

R. Samuel bar R. Gedaliah, the bridegroom, heard that his comrade Master Yehiel the righteous had assented to being slain in the water by his father, he resolved to do likewise. He summoned Menahem, who was the sexton of the synagogue of Cologne, and said to him: 'By your life! Take your sharp sword, inspect it thoroughly lest it be flawed in any manner, and go ahead and cut my throat, lest I have to look upon the death of my comrade. You are to recite the proper blessing before slaughter, and I shall respond, Amen.' This is the way those (two) saints acted; and as they were being slain together, just before they gave up the ghost, they took one another by the hand; and thus they died together in the river, in themselves fulfilling the Scripture (II Sam. 1:23), 'Even in their death they were not divided.' And when R. Samuel the saintly elder, father of R. Yehiel, saw this sanctification which the two young men had carried out, then he too said to the saintly Master Menahem, the sexton: 'Menahem, down with your impulses! Use all your strength now! With the very sword I used on my son Yehiel, slay me! I've inspected it thoroughly and it is without flaw, it will not impair the sacrifice.' Whereupon R. Menahem took the sword in his hand, and after having inspected it thoroughly he cut the throat of R. Samuel the elder as he had done to R. Samuel the bridegroom. Menahem recited the appropriate blessing, and R. Samuel responded after him, 'Amen.' Finally Master Menahem too, that saint of God on high, threw himself on the sword, and it pierced his belly, and there he died. Thus in the water these saints sanctified the Holy Name of Him who is Zealous, of Him who is the Avenger. Come now all you citizens of the world and take a good look: Was there ever *since the days of Adam* an act of Unifying the Name like this!" [18]

With grief, but no less with pride, the chroniclers were conscious of the uniqueness of their generation, which more than all previous

---

[18] NS, p. 19 = Habermann, pp. 45-46.

generations *since the days of Adam* had to endure what is required
in order to sanctify His Great Name in the world. Yet the pattern
of the original Akedah never ceased to hover before their mind's
eye, as though no experience surpassed that one in sanctity. The
victims themselves constantly set before their own eyes the example
of the Patriarchs' behavior on Mount Moriah, and yearned to act
their own parts in the image and likeness of the earlier dramatis
personae.

Thus: In the community of Worms, some eight hundred souls
were killed in the course of two days at the end of the month Iyyar
1096. Among these were some who "offered up sacrifices of righteousness, who with whole heart took their sons and slew them for
the Unification of His Glorious and Awesome Name. . . . Now
there was a unique person there whose name was R. Meshullam
bar Isaac, and in a loud voice he called out to all those standing
by and to his lifelong companion,[19] Mistress Zipporah: 'All ye great
and small, hearken unto me. Here is my son whom God gave me
and to whom my wife Zipporah gave birth *in her old age; Isaac is*
this child's name; and now *I shall offer him up as Father Abraham
offered up his son Isaac.'* Whereupon Zipporah besought him: 'O
my lord, my lord, *do not yet lay thy hand upon the lad* whom I
raised and brought up after having given birth to him *in my old
age.* Slay me first so that I shall not have to behold the death of
the child.' But he replied, saying: 'Not even for a moment shall I
delay, for He who gave him to us will take him away to his own
portion and lay him to rest in Father Abraham's bosom.' *And he
bound his son Isaac, and picked up the knife to slay his son,* and
recited the blessing appropriate for slaughter. And the lad replied,
'Amen.' And the father slew the lad. Then he took his shrieking
wife and *both of them together* left the room; and the vagabonds

---

[19] *Te'omato.*

murdered them. Over such as these, wilt Thou hold Thy peace, O Lord?"[20]

Obviously this account has been drawn up in the very language of the biblical Akedah story. But what was the reality?

Well, whenever we have at our disposal Christian sources also, in a number of instances it is possible to confirm the testimony of the chronicles and poems of those days. One may assume, therefore, that as a rule the reports corresponded to the reality "as much as was humanly possible, and to a greater degree in fact than is the case with other reports in the course of Jewish history."[21]

If this is so, then it is all the more amazing to read countless times in the contemporary sources that both the sacrificers and the very victims of sacrifice saw as the crowning act of their role the performance of the Fathers Abraham and Isaac, as though no trial could be greater than that endured by the Patriarchs. Solomon bar Samson records "on the testimony of the elders"[22] who were eye and ear witnesses to the events of 1096: "And Zion's precious sons, the people of Mainz, were put through the ten trials like Father *Abraham. . . .* They too offered up their sons, *exactly* as Abraham offered up his son Isaac. . . . There were 1,100 victims in one day, every one of them *like the Akedah of Isaac son of Abraham.*"[23] And it is in the same vein when the contemporary *payyetanim*, and the penitential poets, and the writers of dirges take over:

> *Compassionate women, in tears, with their own hands slaughtered,*
> *as at the Akedah at Moriah.*
> *Innocent souls withdrew to eternal life, to their station on high.*

---

[20] NS, p. 50 (and cf. p. 2) = Habermann, p. 96 (and cf. p. 25): *Maaseh ha-Gezerot ha-Yeshanot* "is probably the oldest of the chronicles"; cf. Isaiah Sonne in *REJ*, XCVI (1932), 118ff., and now again in *Zion*, XII (1947), 74ff.

[21] Yizhak Baer, op. cit., p. 6; cf. above, n. 7.

[22] NS, p. 21 = Habermann, p. 48.

[23] NS, pp. 7-8 = Habermann, pp. 31-32.

Let not Your foes triumph! Let the martyrs' blood spatter Your royal purple.[24]

Like a permanent refrain, this comparison of their experience with that of the Patriarchs recurs in all the writings of that generation, and you will find an echo of it in the poetry of R. Ephraim of Bonn:

They offered up sacrifices, they prepared victims like Isaac their Father.[25]

Like Isaac their Father? But was not Isaac delivered from the knife's thrust? Was he not restored to his father very much alive? These pious folk were butchered and became food for the worms! How is it then that from out of the mouths of these votaries and victims, or the relations of the slain, there did not burst forth a painful groan like to that of the saintly mother, bereft of all her sons, as she addressed herself to Father Abraham and, even more, to the deaf-mute heavens—You built one altar and *did not* sacrifice your son, but we built altars in the hundreds and thousands and *did sacrifice* our children on them! Yours was the *trial*, but ours were the *performances!*[26]

Not a hint of this; not a whisper of such thoughts in the records of those times. You will never find that they protest: How compare

---

[24] R. Eliezer bar Nathan; cf. NS, pp. 45-46 = Habermann, p. 81, and notes, p. 252. "Purple": See Yelamdenu, cited by Yalkut *ad* Ps. 110:6, #869 from Yelamdenu, and so accordingly interpret also Midrash Tehilim 9:13; cf. ed. Buber, p. 89; cf. also Bereshit Rabbati, ed. Albeck, p. 176. Such comforting language is favored by the chroniclers and religious poets of the times of the Crusades; cf. Ephraim of Bonn in Sefer Zekirah (NS, p. 65 = Habermann, p. 122); R. Eliezer bar Nathan (above, n. 15);

R. David bar Meshullam (above, n. 13, Habermann, p. 69); Judah bar Kalonymos, *Kobes al Yad*, NS, III, p. 40 (ed. H. Schirmann); R. Menahem bar Jacob, *Sefer ha-Demaot*, I, p. 240 = Habermann, p. 149; R. Baruch bar Samuel of Mainz, *Yediot ha-Makon le-Heker ha-Shirah ha-Ivrit*, of Schocken Institute, VI, p. 133 (ed. Habermann).

[25] NS, 63 = Habermann, p. 120.

[26] Cf. above, ch. II, nn. 7-8.

the one who gave his life to the one who did not have to do so?
At the utmost you will find that they underscore the large number
of victims, but this does not lead them at all to call attention to
the radical difference between the unconsummated offering and the
offering mercilessly brought to completion:

> *He had but one, he hastened to obey.*
> *That merit is on his descendants, time out of mind,*
> *The more so when so many slaughter their children . . .*
> *No altar, no altar-ledge can contain their blood.*
> *Let it atone for Jacob's iniquity!* [27]
>
> *The covenant, the oath*
> *Are well known that You swore to Abraham . . .*
> *If for one offering You granted grace,*
> *All the more for these You will pardon iniquity!* [28]

Are we to suppose that in the consciousness of that generation
the haggadah about Father Abraham took deep roots, that in the
end he did do what would have been almost impossible to defend?
Is it possible that those who did the sacrificing and those who were
the sacrifices in those calamity-laden times imagined that on Mount
Moriah also, at the command of his Creator, the father rose up and
took his son Isaac, bound him, slew him, then burnt his victim,
and the ashes thereof are still in a heap on top of the altar as
stored-up merit and for the atonement of generation after generation
to the end of time . . . ?

[27] *Akedah*, by R. Joel bar Isaac ha-Levi of Bonn: "The Lord puts the righteous to test"; Habermann, p. 112.
[28] See above, n. 1.

IV

*Now when Isaac, lying on top of the altar, heard
the angel say, "Put not forth thy hand," he exclaimed:
"Blessed is He who quickens the dead."* [1]

Early generations had before them a midrash on the Shemoneh
Esreh Prayer [2] which has survived in our sources only in abbreviated
and fragmentary form. The masters of Haggadah undertook to find
in events in the lives of the Patriarchs the basis for the component
elements of that central prayer—something like what the talmudic
Sages did in connection with the benedictions of the Grace-after-
Meals service: "The first benediction, 'He who feeds,' Moses instituted for Israel at the time the manna came down; the benediction
'for the Land' Joshua instituted for them when they entered the
Land; the benediction 'Rebuilder of Jerusalem' David and Solomon
instituted; 'over Israel Thy people and Jerusalem Thy city' David
instituted; and Solomon instituted 'over Thy great and holy
House.'" [3]

Along such lines all the Shemoneh Esreh blessings were also
explained. The first three benedictions were already associated in
very early times with the Three Patriarchs. Thus, the "Shield" bene-

---

[1] Sefer ha-Eshkol, by R. Abraham of
Narbonne, ed. S. and H. Albeck, I, p. 27.
[2] Cf. L. Zunz in *Die gottesdienstlichen
Vorträge der Juden* (Berlin, 1832), p. 272,
and R. David Luria in the introduction
to his commentary on Pirke R. Eliezer
[hereafter abbr. PRE], nn. 7 and 8; and,
above all, Louis Ginzberg, *Commentary
on the Palestinian Talmud*, III, pp. 238ff.
[3] B. Berakot 48b.

diction was instituted in the days of Abraham, when he was saved from the Furnace of Chaldea,[4] or when he defeated the four kings,[5] who were the first in history to have resorted to the sword [6] and the first to bring war into the world. And when he returned safe from battle, "Abraham rose and prayed before the Holy One, blessed be He, and said: Master of the universe, it is not by the might of my hands that I did all these things, but by the might of Thy right hand, for Thou art a *shield* unto me in this world and in the world to come, as it is said (Ps. 3:4), 'But Thou, O Lord, art a *shield* about me,' to wit, in this world; 'my glory and the lifter up of my head' (ibid.), in the world to come. Whereupon the ones on high responded with 'Blessed art Thou, O Lord, shield of Abraham.' "[7] Another tradition has it that it was Abraham himself who recited the "Shield" benediction.

So too with the institution of the Sanctus benediction: "When Father Jacob came upon the gateway to the heavens and sanctified the Name of the Holy One, blessed be He, the ministering angels declared immediately: 'Blessed art Thou, O Lord, the Holy God.' "[8] Another tradition has it that it was Jacob himself who recited the benediction, "the Holy God."[9]

It stands to reason that the benediction which in the order of the Prayers comes second should be attached to the one that is second

[4] Shibbole ha-Leket, Inyan Tefillah 18, ed. S. Buber, 9a; Tanya, Inyan ha-Tefillah, sec. 4 (Cremona, 1565), 7a; R. Mordecai Jaffe's Lebush ha-Tekelet, sec. 112; *Bet ha-Midrash* (Jellinek), V, p. 54.

[5] PRE, end of ch. 27.

[6] Cf. Tanhuma, Lek Leka, 7, and Tanhuma, Lek Leka, ed. Buber, p. 64.

[7] Eshkol, p. 27: "For the Sages say in the Aggadah that when Abraham slew the kings and the Holy One, blessed be He,

said to him, 'I am a shield to thee,' he began to recite: Blessed be the Shield of Abraham."

[8] Shibbole ha-Leket, 9b; cf. PRE, end of ch. 35: "and the celestial ones responded with: Blessed art Thou, Holy God."

[9] Eshkol, loc. cit.: "And when Jacob beheld the angels ascending and descending and there was the Shekinah over him, and they were reciting their acclamations before Him, he began to recite: Blessed be the Holy God."

in the order of the Patriarchs, and thus the "Might" benediction became associated with Isaac. Such an association is most natural, for of all the happenings in Isaac's life nothing was of a finer haggadic weave than the relating of the Akedah to the blessing of *Resurrection*. It is quite likely that in the beginning the exposition remained within the natural bounds of Scripture, along the lines perhaps of the citation from *Sefer ha-Eshkol*, to wit, that when the victim bound on the altar heard the angel of the Lord calling from heaven, "Lay not thy hand upon the lad," he gave thanks imme-diately and recited the benediction, Blessed be He who quickens the dead. It is the same with the passage in the Midrash on the Akedah of Isaac[10]: "Now the moment the knife touched Isaac's throat his soul took flight. . . . Forthwith the Holy One said to Michael: Do not let the father slaughter him! (And the angel) said to Abraham: 'Lay not thy hand upon the lad.' Whereupon Abraham unbound the lad and his soul returned to him; and he stood up on his feet and recited the Resurrection-of-the-dead benediction": that is to say, in terror of that knife Isaac fainted away, and when he came to, he recited the Resurrection benediction.[11]

Then there were others who added touches of the miraculous to the story. "R. Judah says: When the sword touched Isaac's throat his soul flew clean out of him. And when He let His voice be heard from between the two cherubim, 'Lay not thy hand upon the lad,' the lad's soul returned to his body. Then his father unbound him, and Isaac rose, knowing that in this way the dead would come back to life in the future; whereupon he began to recite, Blessed art

---

[10] Michael Higger, *Halakot we-Aggadot* (New York, 1933), p. 72.

[11] Cf. Midrash Wa-Yosha (Jellinek, *Bet ha-Midrash*, I, p. 38): And lo, there was the knife on his throat . . . his soul took wing at once . . . and an angel called. . . . Forthwith he left him alone and his soul returned to him . . . and he recited the benediction, Blessed art Thou, O Lord, who quickenest the dead.

Thou, O Lord, who quickens the dead." [12] But even such a view is not far-fetched, and it seems that such comments were in no way intended to break loose from the limits of the natural. On the contrary, what the homilist seems to be driving at is this: Let no man despair of the Compassion even in the moment when the point of the sword is on his throat, and only the final thrust is next.

Still others chose another moment of the Akedah narrative to focus on, and their exposition is built up on the idiom of the verse (Gen. 27:33), "And Isaac trembled very exceedingly": "No one uses an expression like 'very exceedingly' unless (he is referring to) the fact that before the present terror there had already been one . . . on Mount Moriah. When his father bound him, and took the knife to slay him, the Holy One, blessed be He, revealed Himself to the angels and opened up the heavens. Now Isaac lifted his eyes . . . *and beheld the Holy One, blessed be He, and the Chariot chambers* and the angels—and was seized with trembling." [13] The two haggadic traditions were merged, as we find in the version recorded by R. Judah of Barcelona: "When Father Isaac was on the point of being sacrificed as a freewill whole burnt offering, *he beheld the light of the Shekinah*, and his soul flew out of him, but the Holy

---

[12] PRE, ch. 31 = Yalkut, #101; and cf. MhG *ad* Gen. 22:12 (in R. Eliezer's name).

[13] Tanhuma, ed. Buber, Toledot, 22, p. 141; see also Gen. R. 65:10 *ad* "and his eyes were too dim to see" (Gen. 27:1)— "because of that sight he had; for when Father Abraham subjected Isaac to Akedah, he turned his eyes upward and looked at the Shekinah, and his eyes were dimmed." Cf. also Gen. R. 67:2. And cf. MhG, Gen. 27:1: "He beheld the splendor of the Shekinah and his eyes were dimmed"; cf. PRE, ch. 32.

Sekel Tob, p. 64: "When the sword touched his throat his soul flew up into Paradise, and he beheld the soul of his mother, Sarah, who had died in the interim—because Samael had gone and informed her. . . . His father has already slaughtered him. Whereupon she let out a scream and her soul departed. But when the Holy One, blessed be He, made His voice heard from between the Cherubim, his soul returned to his body, etc. He said: Blessed art Thou, O Lord, who quickenest."

One, blessed be He, revived him. And when he came to his wits and recognized that this is the way the dead will return to life again in the future, he rose to his feet, gave thanks and sang praises before our Creator, and said: Blessed art Thou, O Lord, who quickens the dead." [14]

Sometimes the haggadic interpretation was further embellished by the talmudic Sages with comment on the subject of the dew of light (Isa. 26:19), i.e., the dew of Resurrection: "Where does it come down from? From the head of the Holy One, blessed be He. And in the Age to Come He shakes the hair of His head, and thus brings down the reviving dew and revives the dead." [15] This is the version in the *Midrash Lekah Tob*, and it is set down in connection with the verse (Gen. 31:42), "The God of Abraham and the Fear of Isaac"—"for Isaac was in the grip of fear as he lay bound on top of the altar, and his soul flew out of him, and the Holy One, blessed be He, restored it to him by means of the dewdrops for Resurrection of the dead." [16] Obviously in this haggadic tradition of the dew of resurrection there are additional touches of the miraculous or imaginative highlighting, but there is still no necessary contradiction between the accounts of Scripture and of Midrash.

But then we finally get to that small Midrash on the Prayer in *Shibbole ha-Leket*. On the surface it seems that here have been assembled only the different haggadic strokes we have listed and

[14] Commentary on Sefer Yezirah, p. 125.

[15] PRE, end of ch. 34, perhaps from a midrash on *the Prayer* (Shemoneh Esre). As to "the vivifying dew from heaven in which is the light of the life of the soul," cf. the Responsum of Rab Hai Gaon, *Ozar ha-Geonim*, Sukkah, VI, 2, pp. 72-75 = *Arugat ha-Bosem*, ed. E. E. Urbach, I, 261.

[16] Lekah Tob, ed. Buber, p. 161. I have emended on the basis of MS Adler 437 in the Library of the Jewish Theological Seminary of America. See also R. Joshua ibn Shuaib's *Sefer Derashot*, Wa-Yese pericope: Some explain *"Fear of Isaac"*: he took an oath, By the Akedah! and he called it "Fear of Isaac." Cf. Abraham ibn Ezra *ad* Gen. 31:53: And some say, this "Fear" is an allusion to the Akedah day; and the interpretation is not far-fetched.

outlined thus far; but its language clearly reveals that something
new has been added, and now the profile of the whole midrash is
suddenly transformed in a manner we could never have anticipated
or dreamed of from our reading of Scripture: "When Father Isaac
was bound on the altar and *reduced to ashes and his sacrificial dust
was cast* on to Mount Moriah, the Holy One, blessed be He, immediately brought upon him dew and revived him. That is why
David, may he rest in peace, said: 'Like the dew of Hermon that
cometh down from the mountains of Zion' etc. (Ps. 133:3)—for
he is referring to that dew with which [the Holy One, blessed be
He] revived Father Isaac. Forthwith the ministering angels began
to recite, Blessed art Thou, O Lord, who quickens the dead." [17]

Perhaps this last detail becomes intelligible now: "According to
the later versions of the Haggadah, all the benedictions of the
Prayer were recited by the ministering angels—for a favorite motif
of the later authorities is that of 'the angels' Prayer.' " [18] In this way
the dignity of prayer is enhanced, since thus men address their

[17] Shibbole ha-Leket, 9a-b, on which
Tanya draws; see above, n. 4. "The Holy
One, blessed be He": wanting in Shibbole
ha-Leket. See Naphtali Hirz Treves,
Melakah Hadashah (Commentary on the
Prayer Book, Thiengen, 1560), morning
prayer, end of the Resurrection Benediction: When Isaac had been bound on top
of the altar, *and his ashes had been
heaped up*, the Holy One brought the
dew and revived him. Then the ministering angels began to recite, Blessed art
Thou, O Lord, who quickenest the dead.
And see Zohar, Noah pericope, Tosefta,
60a: "When Isaac was sacrificed on the
altar, his soul which was in him in This
World departed. But when it was said by
Abraham, Blessed be He who quickens
the dead, his soul of the World to Come

came back to him."
   Perhaps J. Berakot 5:2, 9b = J. Taanit
1:1, 63d also alludes to the dew of resurrection. R. Jacob of Kefar Hanan, in the
name of Resh Lakish: When their an-
cestor Abraham did My will, I swore to
him that never would I withdraw the
dew from his descendants. What is the
proof? "To thee the dew of thy youth,"
and immediately after it is written, "The
Lord hath sworn, and will not retract"
(Ps. 110:3f.). Cf. Gen. R. 39:8 and
Theodor *ad loc.*, p. 370, on " 'in the
mountain of holiness' (Ps. loc. cit.), the
eternal mountain," possibly Mount
Moriah.
[18] Ginzberg, *Commentary on the Palestinian Talmud*, III, 261ff.

acclamations to God in angelic speech. Apparently, according to the earliest versions of the Midrash on the Prayer, its benedictions were instituted by the Patriarchs, as accompaniment you might say of the events in *their lives*. But in that case, how could Isaac sing his Creator's praises if he were no longer among the living? The dead do not praise the Lord! Shall we say then that the Resurrection benediction had to be recited by the denizens on high? Not necessarily. For we have already seen that the Haggadah masters had no difficulty attributing the benediction to Isaac—which he recited when seized by panic, either when the knife was coming at him, or at the awesome sight of the light of the Shekinah: and the moment he could catch his breath and come to, he recited Blessed art Thou, O Lord, who quickens the dead.

Or alternatively: One might be tempted to say that there was no peace for the Haggadah until it could magnify the very dimensions of the miraculous, in order to fix firmly the teaching of belief in a literal resurrection of the dead—that this was no figure of speech—and therefore it felt compelled to put Isaac to death and then with the dew of resurrection it proceeded to revive him, so that in his own flesh he personally would witness, and from his experience others would learn, that in this way the dead would come to life again in the future: ergo, the doctrine of the Resurrection of the dead is substantiated by the Torah! [19]

Not at all. Nothing in this haggadic lore even faintly suggests that some polemic against heretics or unbelievers is being contemplated; no doctrinal intention is discernible here. In fact, if you adopt this line of reasoning, the haggadic tradition has made a miserable bargain, and was bound to lose more than it could ever

---

[19] Cf. PRE, ch. 31: "And Isaac came to know *Resurrection of the dead as taught by the Torah*," which is a gloss based on the reading of the Mishnah Sanhedrin, beginning of ch. Helek (10:1).

gain. For this Midrash flatly contradicts Scripture and everything it reports on the subject of the Akedah.

The more you inspect this particular haggadah the more you discover that such could not have been either its intention or its origin. Either something is missing, or something that was originally in this short Midrash on the Prayer has been suppressed. Note well: "When Isaac was bound on the altar"—and how does the text go on? "And was reduced to ashes and his sacrificial dust was cast on to Mount Moriah." Not even a mention of the father *slaying*.

May it not be proposed that the halakic authorities[20] who preserved this Midrash and transmitted it to us sensed the opposition between the account of the Haggadah and the account of the Torah, and sought to diminish that conflict as much as possible? For in Scripture Abraham is explicitly instructed from heaven: "Lay not *thy hand* upon the lad, neither do thou *anything* to him." Perhaps here we arrive at the basis for the omission we have discerned in the version of *Shibbole ha-Leket*. Perhaps the scholars responsible for this wording deliberately omitted from the story of Isaac's death every trace of the knife's movement and every suggestion of a *hand* on the lad. It is as though they strove to uproot any possible notion which might lead readers to suspect that Abraham had rebelled against his God's commandment, or had in any way deviated from what is laid down in the Torah. Indeed, the very reverse! When Abraham heard the words "Lay not thy hand," he at once pulled his hand away from his son Isaac—and if something happened after all, the fault was not his. "And (Isaac) was reduced to ashes and his sacrificial dust was cast on to Mount Moriah": obviously the flames of the fire were already licking away at the one bound on top of the woodpile, and in the twinkling of an eye he was turned into hissing embers and hot ash . . .

[20] See above, n. 4.

For indeed the words of this haggadah are confirmed and reinforced by another text: "And he bound Isaac his son, and laid him on the altar on top of the wood" (Gen. 22:9). What is the meaning of "on top of"? [21] "On top of the sacrificial woodpile." [22] "This teaches that he arranged the wood the way the woodpile on the altar is arranged. Here (Gen. 22:9) it is written, 'And (Abraham) laid the wood in order,' and elsewhere (Lev. 1:7), '(And the sons of Aaron) shall lay wood in order upon the fire.' " [23] In the Akedah account in Scripture there is no mention of laying out the fire. Not so in the Midrash: "And (Abraham) laid out *the fire* and the wood." [24] As is their way, the talmudic Sages believed that not one iota of the priestly law did Abraham neglect. What is the proper order for the whole burnt offering? "And the sons of Aaron the priest shall put *fire* upon the altar, and lay *wood* in order *upon the fire*" (Lev. 1:7): (that is,) *"Wood* upon the fire, and not fire upon the wood." [25] If that is the case, then Abraham offered up his sacrifice in accordance with the proper order for making a whole burnt offering, and he did with the wood what is done in the proper laying-out of the sacrificial woodpile, wood on top of the fire, and he put his son "on top of the wood." And if in fact he *did not do anything* to the lad and did not remove him speedily from the wood upon the fire that was burning, why, in a twinkling the whole pile went up in a blaze and the flames of fire had Isaac to themselves and "he was reduced to ashes" and dust.

At any rate, one thing is clear: it was not the author of the Midrash on the Eighteen benedictions of the Prayer who invented

---

[21] Cf. Tanhuma, ed. Buber, Wa-Yera, 41, and Yalkut, #101.

[22] Sekel Tob, p. 62.

[23] MhG *ad* 22:9, p. 354.

[24] PRE, ch. 31. And see the version published by Michael Higger in *Horeb* (New York), X (1948), 195; cf. R. David Luria, nn. 39 and 59. And observe the idiom of the haggadah in *Sepher ha-Pardes*, ed. Ehrenreich, p. 316: "Isaac was bound *on top of the fire.*" Cf. below, R. Ephraim's *Akedah*, line 47.

[25] Sifra, ed. Weiss, 7a, end.

the Haggadah on the burning up and resurrection of Isaac. That haggadah antedates our author, and he simply used it for his own needs, to explain how and when the Resurrection benediction of the Prayer was instituted. Not only that, but very possibly in the earliest and original version of the midrash, Isaac's death was not mentioned at all. Clearly therefore, the root and origin of the haggadic tradition that Isaac was slain or burnt and then rose from the dead are not to be located in the late Midrash on the Prayer.*

---

* [And now, thanks to a Cambridge University Library manuscript (Or. 1080, Box I:48), we learn that the *Shibbole ha-Leket* reading is indeed abridged. Perhaps either R. Zedekiah bar Abraham delli Mansi or some pious soul of an earlier generation was exercising restraint—for reasons similar to those which prompted R. Isaac Aboab to omit that haggadah entirely from beginning to end. For this MS reads: "When Abraham bound his son Isaac on the altar, *and slew him and burned him*, (the lad) was reduced to ashes, and his ashes were cast on Mount Moriah; then the Holy One, blessed be He, brought down life-giving dew and revived him. That is why David said, 'Like Hermon dew which descends.' This is a reference to the dew with which the Holy One, blessed be He, revived Father Isaac. (Whereupon) the ministering angels proceeded to say: *Blessed be He who quickens the dead.*" See S. Spiegel in the *Abraham Weiss Jubilee Volume* (New York, 1964), pp. 553-566.]

V

*O, do Thou regard the ashes of Father Isaac
heaped up on top of the altar, and deal with Thy children
in accordance with the Mercy Attribute.*[1]

The great importance which the Akedah possesses already led the
Haggadah masters of the earliest generations to devote their exegetical
skill to the theme of the ram substituted for Isaac; they could not
rest until they had included it in the list of things created on the first
Sabbath eve at twilight.[2] For had it not been for this substitute that
God provided in place of Abraham's son, Isaac would never have
had offspring, nor could the covenant and the promise have been
fulfilled (Gen. 21:12), "For it is through Isaac that offspring shall
be continued for you." However, since Isaac was redeemed, it is
as though all Israel had been redeemed.[3] This is why that ram was
prized so, the ram that Abraham offered up as a burnt offering in
place of his son; and through it a multitude of miracles came to
pass, the greatest of which was: it too, after being slaughtered,
returned to life!—for "the Holy One, blessed be He, restored it to
its original state."[4] On the face of it, this haggadah is also amazing,

---

[1] Supplication for the one who sounds the shofar: Mahzor, ed. Heidenheim (Vienna, 1827), 80a = *Ozar ha-Tefillot*, 523b.

[2] Abot 5:6, B. Pesahim 54a: Ten things were created on the (first) Sabbath eve at twilight, etc. R. Josiah says in his

father's name: The ram also.

[3] J. Taanit 2:4, 65d: cf. L. Ginzberg, *Yerushalmi Fragments*, p. 176.

[4] R. Bahya on Exod. 19:13, and from here in Isaac Karo, *Toledot Yizhak*. See Ginzberg, *Legends*, V, p. 252.

like the haggadah of Isaac's resurrection, although it is easier to understand the origins of the ram's revival.

In the first generation of the Tannaim, R. Hanina ben Dosa already held forth as follows: "That ram, not a part of it went to waste: its tendons became the ten strings of the harp that David used to play on; its skin became the leather girdle around the loins of Elijah; as to its horns, with the left one the Holy One, blessed be He, sounded the alarum at Mount Sinai; and with the right one, which is larger than the left, He will in the future sound the alarum at the Ingathering of the Exiles in the Age to Come." [5]

Taking his cue from this midrash which occurs in *Pirke de-R. Eliezer*, Rashi offered the following interpretation of the clause in Exodus (19:13), "When the ram's horn sounds a long blast" on Mount Sinai: "That was the horn of the ram substituted for Isaac." [6] Both in regard to this midrash and to Rashi's interpretation, all kinds of questions were raised long ago. [7] Was not that ram Abraham substituted for his son Isaac a whole burnt offering?—and is it not said (Lev. 1:9), "And the priest shall turn *the whole* into smoke on the altar as a burnt offering, an offering by fire of pleasing odor to the Lord"?—and did not the talmudic Sages teach: "The whole" includes the bones *and the tendons and the horns* and the hooves? [8] Such being the case, the tendons of that ram must surely have been consumed; how could they later serve as the strings of David's harp? The ram's horns too were consumed; how could they be used later for sounding the alarum either at the Mount Sinai convocation or in the distant future at the Gathering Together of the Exiles?

There were some naturally who tried to solve this problem by

[5] PRE, ch. 31; Yalkut, #101 and #436 in Isaiah 27:13; MhG, Gen. 22:13.
[6] Rashi on the Torah (Pentateuch; 2nd edn., A. Berliner, p. 145).

[7] Nahmanides, Jethro pericope, *ad loc.*
[8] Mishnah Zebahim 9:5 and the Talmud *ad loc.*, 86a.

assuming that before the actual offering was made, the tendons
and horns fell from the ram's body and therefore never went up in
smoke—or perhaps they dropped from the altar and were not put
back on.[9] But this is stretching *pilpul* to its limits. Hence they
preferred to imagine instead, "Perhaps the Holy One, blessed be
He, kneaded together the dust (ashes?) of the ram's horns and
restored them to their former state."[10] This is how the haggadah
came into being: the ram Abraham offered up was indeed completely consumed as a burnt offering unto the Lord, but out of its
very ashes it was restored anew, miraculously.

And long before, the Tannaim and the Amoraim had plenty to
argue about regarding that ram. "R. Eliezer says: That ram came
from the mountains where it had been grazing. R. Joshua says:
An angel fetched it from the Garden of Eden, where it had been
grazing under the Tree of Life and drinking from the waters that
course by."[11] That ram was also a subject for difference of opinion
on the part of "R. Judah and R. Yose, one saying, That ram fortunately happened along at the right moment; and the other saying,
That ram was the bellwether of Abraham's flock, and its name was
Isaac; but Abraham failed to recognize it. Said the Holy One,
blessed be He, *Let Isaac for Isaac come*."[12] And similarly "Rab
and Samuel; one said, That ram came along from Abraham's estate
but he did not recognize it; and the other said, That ram grew up
inside the firmament and it was called Isaac."[13] And in R. Isaac's
name this view is handed down: "Abraham had a ram, the bell-

---

[9] To the question of Eliahu Mizrahi (on
Rashi), R. Abraham A. Gombiner replied;
cf. Zayit Raanan on Yalkut, #101; and
so too R. David Luria in his commentary
on PRE, ch. 31, n. 70, who even tried
to find some basis for this—since the ram
was caught in the thicket by his horns
and tried to break free of them, the horns
came loose and could easily fall off.

[10] See above, n. 7.

[11] Yalkut, #101.

[12] MhG *ad* Gen. 22:13, p. 356.

[13] Midrash Composed under the Holy
Spirit, Mann, p. 67.

wether of his flock, whose name was Isaac, and Gabriel rushed and brought it before Abraham, and then Abraham offered it as a burnt offering in place of his son." [14]

"Let Isaac for Isaac come." Perhaps therefore *the ashes of Isaac* are nothing other than the ashes of that ram called Isaac which served as the substitute burnt offering for Isaac son of Father Abraham? Or shall we say perhaps that in a general sense the burnt offering of ram was found acceptable before the Lord, "and it was regarded as Isaac"; [15] or the ashes of the ram which served as sur-rogate suggested that it was *as though* Isaac himself had been burned, and therefore they were called Isaac's ashes? Then this can all be explained along the lines adopted by R. Eleazar ben Pedat, "Although Isaac did not die, Scripture accounts it to him *as though* he had died and his ashes lay on top of the altar." [16]

Indeed, you will often find this guarded expression *as though* recurring in the sources which refer to the ashes of Isaac, *as though* the expression were eager to dull somewhat the sharp edge of the startling phrase, to soften its effect, to reduce it to mere figure of speech or metaphor: " 'Then will I remember My covenant with Jacob, and also My covenant with Isaac, also My covenant with Abraham will I remember' (Lev. 26:42). Now, why does the verb 'remember' appear along with the names of Abraham and Jacob, but not alongside the name of Isaac? Because his ash is regarded *as*

---

[14] S. Taussig, Neweh Shalom, p. 51.

[15] Sefer ha-Yashar, p. 81. See also Daat Zekenim, 11a: One learns from the Midrash that when the Holy One, blessed be He, said to him, 'Don't lay thy hand,' Abraham refused to put it down until the Holy One, blessed be He, swore to him *that before Him the ashes of the ram would be regarded as though they were Isaac's ashes*, and He swore it to him.

Cf. Yalkut Reubeni (in the name of Asarah Maamarot, 34a): "At the time of the Akedah, Isaac's soul quit him and went over to the ram which had been created on the (first Sabbath eve) twilight. And this is the meaning of 'the sheep for His burnt offering, my son' (Gen. 22:8), that sheep is my son, actually."

[16] MhG ad Gen. 22:19.

though it were heaped up on top of the altar." [17] "Whenever the children of Isaac sin and as a result come into distress, let there be recalled to their credit the Akedah of Isaac and let it be regarded by Thee *as though* his ashes were heaped up on top of the altar, and do Thou forgive them and redeem them from their distress." [18]

And yet, here too it seems that things are not so easily to be explained or explained away. We have been taught: "What is the proper order for public fasts? The ark is to be taken out to the broadway of the city, and on top of the ark real ashes are to be placed. R. Yudan son of R. Manasseh and R. Samuel bar Nahman: one said, the ashes were intended to recall the merit of Abraham; and the other said, they were intended to recall the merit of Isaac. He who says that they were intended to recall Abraham's merit (believes that it is immaterial if on top of the ark) either dust (*'fr*) or real ashes (*'fr*) be placed—take note of 'And I am dust and ashes' (Gen. 18:27). He who says that the ashes were intended to recall Isaac's merit (believes that on top of the ark) only real ashes are to be placed—(for) Isaac's ashes are regarded *as though* they were heaped on top of the altar." [19]

And here is how it is put in the Babylonian Talmud: [20] "Why now are ashes placed on the head of each and every one (of the par-

[17] Sifra, Behukkotai (ed. Weiss, 112c); Lev. R. 36:5; Tanhuma, Toledot, 7 (end) and Gen. R. 94:5: And the Sages say: He looks upon Isaac's ashes *as though* they were heaped up on top of the altar. Rashi *ad* Lev. 26:42: Isaac's ashes appear before Me lying in a heap on the altar. Cf. Rashi *ad* Gen. 22:14: 'On the Mount of the Lord will be seen' Isaac's ashes in a heap set for atonement.

[18] Tanhuma, Wa-Yera, 23 (end) and parallels. Cf. Jellinek, *Bet ha-Midrash*, V, p. 157: Abraham requested of the Holy One, blessed be He, that so long as Israel make mention of Isaac's Akedah before Him, it continue to serve as an atonement for them, *as though* (Isaac) had been burned up on top of the altar. Cf. Minhat Yehudah, Wa-Yera pericope, 11a: Do Thou swear to me that Isaac's ashes will be heaped up before Thee as a memorial for all time, *as though* I had sacrificed him.

[19] M. Taanit 2:1, J. Taanit, 65a. Cf. Gen. R. 49:11.

[20] B. Taanit 16a.

ticipants)? There is a difference of opinion in this matter on the part of R. Levi bar Hama and R. Hanina. One says (All the participants put ashes on their heads, to indicate thereby,) Before Thee we are all [like dust and] ashes; and the other says (That is done) so that He might call to mind for our sake Isaac's ashes."

This summoning up remembrances of Isaac's ashes in the ritual of the public fasts is symbolic in the full sense of the word: it is a testimony to the belief or to the haggadic tradition that Isaac was offered up as a whole burnt offering, and of his remains nothing was left on top of the altar except his ashes. Or—shall we say this is no more than figure of speech and poetic license?

In connection with the plague that took place in the days of David, it is said (I Chron. 21:15): "And God sent an angel unto Jerusalem to destroy it; and as he was about to destroy, the Lord beheld, and He repented Him of the evil, and said to the destroying angel: It is enough; now stay thy hand." "What was it the Lord *beheld*? Said Rab: He beheld Father Jacob, as it is written (Gen. 32:3), 'And Jacob said when he *beheld* them: This is God's camp.' And Samuel said: It was the ashes of Isaac He beheld, as it is said (Gen. 22:8), 'God will for Himself behold the lamb for a burnt offering, my son.' " [21] And like the latter view is the Targum, the Aramaic version, of that Chronicles verse: "He beheld the ashes of the Akedah of Isaac in the foundation of the altar."

Where is that altar located? Is it perhaps only the altar in heaven? Come now, listen: When the generation that returned from the Babylonian Exile began to build the Second Temple, "How did they know what to do with the altar? Said R. Eleazar: They beheld the altar all built and Michael, the Great Prince, stood by it sacrificing on it. But R. Isaac Napha said: *They beheld Isaac's ashes, that these*

[21] B. Berakot 62b.

lay on that spot." [22] Clearly, then, we are dealing with the altar on earth, and the language of the text cannot be watered down or deprived of its literal meaning. Manifestly they did believe "that the ashes of Isaac have been hidden away forever, and the Holy One, blessed be He, remembers those ashes, and shows them to His children, and so too at the building of the Second Temple He showed them those ashes. Thus they discovered the right location; and by Isaac's merit they were able to build the altar on its proper base. And the same applies to the time for the First Temple structure, when the destroying angel struck—the Holy One, blessed be He, looked upon those ashes as a reminder, as it is written, 'And as he was about to destroy, the Lord beheld' " and so on[23]—exactly like Samuel's interpretation.

There is no doubt about it. The haggadah about the ashes of Isaac who was consumed by fire like an animal sacrifice, and of whose remains nothing was left except the sacrificial ash, is ancient indeed, and its traces are already visible in the first generation of the Amoraim, in the days of that astronomer Samuel, if not earlier. And you learn from the circle of R. Johanan's disciples, from the report of R. Isaac, that in their days they believed that Isaac's ashes were the foundation of the altar.[24] This being so, the haggadah therefore did not spring up for the first time in the Middle Ages, that "Isaac was reduced to sacrificial ash and his ashes were cast on to Mount Moriah" [25]—although, to be sure, just that version of the haggadic lore became the favorite one in medieval times, possibly because with a little ingenuity one could force it into agreement with the biblical account.

---

[22] B. Zebahim 62a. Cf. PRE, ch. 31, on the ram's ashes serving as the base for the interior altar.

[23] Judah of Barcelona, Commentary on Sefer Yezirah, p. 109.

[24] See above, n. 22.

[25] Shibbole ha-Leket, Inyan Tefillah, 18.

VI

Isaac said to him: Father, have no fears.
May it be His will that one quarter of my blood
serve as an atonement for all Israel.[1]

"The Sages of blessed memory say: If Abraham had not delayed in order to inspect the knife, Isaac would have been slaughtered. . . . How do we know that he inspected the knife? . . . Count the consonants 'wykh 'et hm'aklt' (and he took the knife, Gen. 22:10) and you will find that they are twelve, corresponding to the number of inspections a slaughtering knife must have. . . . But Abraham delayed in order to inspect the knife. Immediately the Holy One, blessed be He, was stirred with compassion for Isaac,"[2] and He told the angel to deliver him, "and he said, Lay not thy hand upon the lad" (Gen. 22:12). Why did the angel refer to the *hand* and not to the knife? (For from the eyes) of the ministering angels tears dropped onto the knife, and it dissolved[3] completely and evaporated.[4] Said Abraham: Perhaps (this has happened because the lad) is not fit to be a sacrificial gift. May I strangle him, may I burn him, shall I cut him up in pieces before Thee? Said He

---

[1] Neweh Shalom, p. 50 = MhG, Gen. 22:8, p. 353 = Mann, p. 66 = Bereshit Rabbati, ed. Albeck, p. 90.

[2] Tanhuma, Saw, 13; cf. B. Hullin 17b.

[3] Gen. R. 56:7: "and he was *shoheb* like wax," i.e., melting away; "why is your body *shoheb*, melting away, on you," Tanhuma, ed. Buber, Toledot, 15, p. 134.

[4] MhG *ad* Gen. 22:12.

to him: "Lay not thy hand!" Said Abraham to Him: In that event,
I have come here in vain. Let me bruise him, let me extract some
blood from him, let me remove from him one *drop of blood!* Said
He to him: "Don't you do anything (*meumah*) to him," don't you
bruise (*mumah*) him.[5]

Clearly then, the Midrash again and still again emphasizes what
is specifically reported by Scripture too, that Abraham was categorically and in no uncertain terms forbidden from heaven so much
as to touch Isaac with evil intent, or remove from him even one drop
of blood. That is why wonder grows by leaps and bounds when
we read in the early sections of Mekilta de-R. Simeon ben Yohai:
"R. Joshua says: 'And God spoke to Moses and said to him, I am
the Lord' (Exod. 6:2)—Said the Holy One, blessed be He, to
Moses, I can be trusted to reward Isaac son of Abraham, *for he left
one quarter of his blood on top of the altar*, and I said to him,
'According to the greatness of thy power I shall set free the offspring appointed to death' (Ps. 79:11), and I wish to take them
out of Egypt. Yet you say to Me, 'Please, O Lord, make someone
else Thine agent' "[6] (Exod. 4:13)!

[5] Lev. R. 20:2: In his heart Abraham kept
pondering, thinking, God forbid, has some
imperfection been discovered in him and
his blood has not been found acceptable?
Cf. the commentary on the Long Tur by
R. Jacob ben Asher (Hanover, 1839), *ad*
Gen. 22:12: "The Midrash has it that
suddenly, gazing at his hand, he saw that
it had no knife. He thought: Perhaps
(the lad) is not fit for sacrifice. And he
sought to strangle him." Cf. Gen. R., on
Gen. 22:12; Pesikta R. 171a; Mann, p.
67; MhG, loc. cit.; Neweh Shalom, p.
51; Midrash Ner ha-Sekalim in M.M.
Kasher, *Torah Shelemah*, IV, p. 896. And
see the Midrash cited in Hadar Zekenim
and Minhat Yehudah, Wa-Yera pericope,

12a: Abraham said to the Holy One,
blessed be He, I'll strangle him; *and may
I trouble You to request Sarah to give
birth to another Isaac for me*, in fulfill-
ment of Your promise to me (Gen. 21:
12), "For it is through Isaac that offspring
shall be continued for you." Cf. Midrash
Tehilim, p. 489.

[6] Mekilta Simeon, ed. D. Hoffman, p. 4;
idem, MhG, Exodus, p. 48. Cf. S. Wert-
heimer, *Ozar Midrashim Kitbe Yad* (Jerusalem, 1913), I, p. 62: "Moses, I can
be depended upon to reward Isaac ben
Abraham, *from whom a quarter of blood
came out* on top of the altar." As for
Resurrection of the dead in this section

This is the kind of midrashic exegesis that can blow the top off everything said in the Torah about the Akedah event. "A quarter *of blood*" did you say! So then, the father did indeed lay hand and knife to the lad, and did do what he did to extract from him a quarter of blood, which is the amount required to keep a man alive, "as that Galilean taught in Rab Hisda's presence—The Holy One, blessed be He, said: Into you I have put a quarter of blood, on the subject of blood I have cautioned you, etc. If you obey them, fine; otherwise I'll have your lives." [7] If, therefore, Isaac gave a quarter *log* of his blood on the altar, then evidently Abraham did not refrain from this mighty strange action, and wound he did, and possibly with his own hands did slaughter his son. Or in Abraham ibn Ezra's language, in his commentary (Gen. 22:19) : The father acted "contrary to Scripture," "for he slaughtered and abandoned" Isaac on the altar.

Nor is that all. Perhaps one may even derive from the verse R. Joshua interpreted (Ps. 79:11), "Let the groaning of the *one in fetters* come before Thee; according to the greatness of Thy power *set free the offspring appointed to death*," that the Holy One, blessed be He, set free the groaning one in fetters, i.e., Isaac who was bound, from his appointment unto death, and revived him with dew for resurrection of the dead? The fact is that what one Midrash puts under lock and key another Midrash opens up: [8] "The Holy

---

(Exod. 6:2), cf. Yelamdenu in Tanhuma, Wa-Era, 1, and Mann, I, p. 384.

[7] B. Shabbat 31b (end) and cf. B. Sotah 5a: If the sea, which has any number of quarts and quarts, can become ugly when even only a light wind gets to blowing, how much the more a human being, in whom there is only one quarter. See further Tosafot *ad loc.*, s.v. *'adam:* R. Hananel explained: The clear blood [in the heart] from which the heart gets

its flow weighs only 25 *sela'im*, which equals a quarter of a *log*. And so too in Aruch, s.v. *rb'*. Professor Saul Lieberman called my attention to the explanation given in the Tosefta (Ahilot 3:2): "Abba Saul says, The amount of blood in a child at the beginning is a quarter (of a *log*)." See also Lieberman, *Tosefet Rishonim*, III, p. 99.

[8] Pesikta Kahana, ch. 32, 200b (ed.

One, blessed be He, will in the future revive the dead by merit of Isaac who offered himself on top of the altar, as it is said (Ps. 102:21), 'To hear the groaning of the one in fetters, to *open up release* for the offspring appointed to death.' "

But it may also be that these verses can be interpreted in still other ways, namely, that the Lord heard the groaning of Isaac who was in fetters, at the time he was hemorrhaging "from the incision as the father began to slaughter him," [9] and He ordered Abraham to *release* him from the fetters and to *leave* the lad the remainder of his life.

Some support for this interpretation may perhaps be furnished by the Midrashim in which a hint of that measure of a quarter of blood at Isaac's Akedah survives and escaped suppression. For example: "And Abraham bound him on the altar and then took the knife in order to slaughter him, until a quarter of *his* blood left him." [10] Or in an anonymous Midrash: "And there were Abraham's eyes on Isaac's eyes, and Isaac's eyes on the very heavens, and tears falling, pouring, from Abraham's eyes until he stood virtually to his height in a pool of tears. He said to Isaac: My son, since you have already begun to give up a quarter of *your* blood, may your Creator appoint some other victim in your place." [11]

In an old Midrash [12] this entire homily is given over in the name of one of the earliest Palestinian Amoraim, a contemporary of Rabbi (Judah the Prince) : " 'And God put Abraham to the test.' Said R. *Yose ben Zimrah:* When the Holy One, blessed be He, said to Abraham, Offer him up as a burnt offering before Me, Abraham came home [and said] to Sarah: How long [is] your son [Isaa]c to

Buber). See Israel Levi in *REJ*, LXIII (1912), 129ff.

[9] Cf. n. 18 in the Prologue, above.

[10] Tanhuma, Wa-Yera, 23.

[11] Yalkut, #101.

[12] Mann, Midrash Composed under the Holy Spirit, p. 65, and note what he writes, p. 45, about the date of this Midrash.

hang on to your apron strings? [I]s he not after all thirty-se[ven y]ears old? He hasn't attended sc[ho]ol, I haven't let him go to the schoolmaster's. [C]ome now, fix provisions for our journ[ey], for he and I are off to the Great Study House. 'So they went both of them together' (Gen. 22:8). What is the meaning of 'together'? Abraham thought, Isaac may take to his legs and run [off]."[13] (Now) Isaac said to his father: Father, 'Behold the fire and the wood; [but where is the lamb for a burnt offering]?' (v. 7) Whereupon Abraham began to ponder: What shall I tell my son Isaac? Forthwith Abraham said to Isaac: Before the Holy One, blessed be He, it is manifest and known that you are 'the lamb for a burnt offering' (ibid.). At that Isaac put his hands to his head and began to cry out, and he wept bitterly. He said to Abraham: Father, Father, so this is the Torah you talked about to my mother Sarah when you said, I am going to take him to the schoolmaster's! Whereupon Abraham began weeping, and he pulled at the hair of his head and beard. And when Isaac beheld his father Abraham (in that state), he said to him: Father, do not be distressed. Come now and carry out the will of your Father in heaven: may it be His will that *a quarter of my blood serve as an atonement for Israel.*"[14]

It is not surprising that, in the extant sources, the midrashic expositions on the subject of the quarter of Isaac's blood agree and correspond in the end with the Scriptural account. That is to be expected. On the contrary, what is surprising is that any trace at all of the haggadah contradicting the Torah has survived. And if

[13] This is the source for MhG, loc. cit. *ad* Gen. 22:8. Cf. Abraham ibn Ezra *ad* Gen. 22:4: Lest Isaac becoming aware *run away* . . . for his father hid the secret from him . . . for had he told it to him . . . it is quite possible *that he would have run away.*

[14] And cf. MhG, loc. cit., and Neweh

Shalom, p. 50: May it be God's will that the quarter of my blood be accepted favorably. Bereshit Rabbati, p. 90: Father, have no fears. May it be His will that the whole quarter of my blood will be favorably accepted before Him who commanded you concerning me.

in fact the fountainhead of words like these is the Mekilta de-R. Simeon ben Yohai, and they were uttered by R. Joshua ben Hananiah, clearly then this haggadah was well known in the second generation of the Tannaim, namely, that Abraham did not recoil nor did he part from the lad until he drew from him a quarter of blood; but it was the Holy One, blessed be He, who had compassion and showed grace to Isaac, and brought about either his recovery from sickness, or his revival. If this be true, then the core of the haggadah is hoary with age, and it was not in the Middle Ages that it first saw the light of day.

VII

"And when he was about to destroy, the Lord beheld"
(I Chron. 21:15). What did He behold?
He beheld the blood at the Akedah of Isaac.[1]

Twice in the Mekilta de-Rabbi Ishmael there appears a very interesting, even surprising statement; and from this statement later generations learned how to eliminate anthropomorphic conceptions and the kind of imagery which might detract from the proper respect due to Heaven.[2] That statement is also instructive for the subject of the Akedah:

" 'And when He seeth the blood' (Exod. 12:23). R. Ishmael used to say: But is not everything manifest and known before Him, as it is said (Dan. 2:22), 'He knoweth what is in the darkness and the light dwelleth with Him,' and it says (Ps. 139:12), 'Even the darkness is not too dark for Thee.' Why then does the Scripture say, 'And when He seeth the blood'? Because it wishes to teach that He reveals Himself and protects them as a reward for even [a single] commandment which they carry out, as it is said (Exod. 12:23), 'And the Lord will pass over the door.' Now, 'passing over' is

---

[1] Mekilta, Bo, 7 and 12, ed. Friedmann, 8a and 12a = ed. Lauterbach, I, pp. 57 and 88.

[2] Moslem scholars mocked and railed at Exod. 12:23, among other verses, as though the Eye on High were short-sighted and depended on signs from flesh and blood. Cf. L. Strauss, "The Ways of Moslem Polemics," *Memorial Volume of the Rabbinical Seminary of Vienna* (Jerusalem, 1946), p. 188, #24.

nothing other than protection, as it is said (Isa. 31:5), 'As birds hovering, so will the Lord of hosts protect Jerusalem; He will deliver it as He protecteth it, He will rescue it as He passeth over.' [Another interpretation of][3] 'And when He seeth the blood': He sees the blood of Isaac's Akedah, as it is said (Gen. 22:14), 'And Abraham called the name of the place The Lord Seeth.' Now, elsewhere (I Chron. 21:15) it says, 'And as he was about to destroy, the Lord beheld, and He repented Him of the evil.' What did He behold? He beheld the blood of Isaac's Akedah, as it is said (Gen. 22:8), 'God will for Himself behold the lamb for a burnt offering.' "[4]

Let me have your attention: It may be that here we have a clue for the original meaning of Passover and the original season of the Akedah. "Passing over is nothing other than *protection*" (*ḥyys* or *ḥswt*), and the paschal sacrifice with the putting of the animal's blood on the houses is nothing other than a typical apotropaic sacrifice of cleansing and *protection*. Like that mark which was set on the foreheads (cf. Ezek. 9) of the righteous in Jerusalem, "so that the angels of destruction might have no power over them," [5] so also the blood of the paschal offering which was put on the two doorposts and the lintel of the houses was intended as a protection and deliverance from demons. Blood has both a terrorizing and redemptive potency; it can terrify the destroyer and can drive off the demonic from human habitation. Such concepts and customs are nourished from the regions of idolatry, and their roots go deep into primitive notions of prebiblical times, long before the religion of Israel.[6]

[3] So the reading in Yalkut, Exod. #200.

[4] See above, n. 1.

[5] B. Shabbat 55a.

[6] W. Robertson Smith, *Lectures on the Religion of the Semites*[2] (London, 1894), pp. 464f.; J. G. Frazer, *The Golden Bough*, IV (New York, 1935), pp. 172ff.; S. H. Hooke, *The Origins of Early Semitic Ritual* (London, 1938), pp. 48ff.; Joh. Pedersen, "Passafest und Passalegende," *ZAW*, 1934, pp. 161ff.; idem,

The paschal-offering ritual in the Torah is based on a rejection of the primitive practices of paganism, or at least on their transfiguration. And yet, in the sources and in the customs there survives something of the dread of the ancient festival of the first born. The night of the full moon, in the first month of the Spring season and according to the archaic calendar the first of the months of the year, was a time of attack and atonement for members of the tribe. It was the time to appease higher powers, and it was a time to battle against the forces of evil which station themselves on the threshold of the new year in order to harass and hurt man and everything he possesses. It may be, however, that the gods will be placated, and for the price of a small gift of first fruits and first born they will show favor and spare the rest of earth's produce and the cattle litter and the fruit of the womb. By paying a ransom to his gods from the yield of the field and the firstlings and from whatever he plants for food, the primitive hopes to obtain in return the favor that they shall neither hurt nor destroy field and orchard, cattle and property, wives and children. As with the first fruits of his fields, so he delivers to the gods their share of his newborn, the first issue of every animal and human womb, lest the other cattle and children be destroyed. This is the soil out of which grows the offering of first born, human and animal, in the Spring festival of ancient shepherds and herdsmen—all for the purpose of protecting and guarding the tribe and its livestock.

Scripture forbade the sacrifice of the human first born, and for the practice substituted that of the redemption of sons—but the primitive demand of "You shall give Me the first born among your sons" was never actually abolished, for the whole Levitical institution was based on that ancient principle of the sanctity of all first

---

Israel, III-IV (1947), pp. 410ff.; Yehezkel Kaufmann, *Toledot ha-Emunah be-*   *Yisrael*, I, Part 2, p. 547, and II, Part 2, p. 430.

born, "the first issue of every womb among the children of Israel." [7]
The biblical paschal sacrifice also came to put an end to the
heathenish practices of the Spring festival, to abolish human sacrifice and in its place to substitute animal sacrifice. Nevertheless,
here and there vestiges of the age-old heritage did survive, from
strata of the religion of archaic times, before the ancients had yet
learned how to propitiate the gods without resorting to blood sacrifices.

Now, what connection is there between Passover and Isaac's
Akedah?

In ancient times there were two new years on Israel's calendar,
one in the Spring month of Nisan and the other in the Autumn-
ingathering month of Tishri. That cycle where Nisan occurs as the
first of all the months [8] testifies to the antiquity of a New Year in
the Spring. Indeed, that ancient form of calendrical order persisted
in the cultic and royal institutions, for these are conservative by
nature; and as late as Second Temple times the first of Nisan was
still regarded as the beginning of the New Year for the crown, the
correct sequence of the Pilgrimage festivals, and the Shekel offerings. [9] On the other hand, the Feast of Ingathering falls at the end
of the year or turn of the year, [10] which is the beginning of the rainy
season or the beginning of the agricultural year. And this scheme
is preserved in connection with everything attached to the soil and
its cultivation: the first of Tishri is the New Year for determining
sabbatical and jubilee years, for laws affecting fruits of the tree,
vegetable products, and relevant tithes. [11]

Both these New Years were in operation, simultaneously, in

---

[7] Exod. 13:1 and 22:28, Num. 3:12, and
I Kings 8:14ff. Cf. Martin Buber, "Zum
Moloch Problem," *Theologische Blätter,*
XV (1936), 217-224; *Das Königtum
Gottes*, pp. 224ff.

[8] Exod. 12:2.

[9] Mishnah and Tosefta, Rosh ha-Shanah
1:1.

[10] Exod. 23:15, 34:22.

[11] M. Rosh ha-Shanah 1:1, Tosefta 1:8.

rivalry with each other; in the literature of the talmudic Rabbis there are distinct echoes of the contest between Spring and Autumn. *"Tanya*—it has been taught in a tannaite tradition—R. Eliezer says: The world was created in Tishri, in Tishri the Patriarchs were born, in Tishri the Patriarchs died" and so on. "R. Joshua says: The world was created in Nisan, in Nisan the Patriarchs were born, in Nisan the Patriarchs died" and so on.[12]

The Akedah is similarly subject to controversy. Some wished to dignify Tishri with it. " 'In the seventh (*shevii*) month' (Lev. 23:24): R. Berekiah used to refer to it as the Oath (*Shevuata*) month, for in it the Holy One, blessed be He, swore to Father Abraham, may he rest in peace, as it is written (Gen. 22:16), 'And he said, By Myself I swear, the Lord declares.' "[13] This view spread among the people because the sounding of the ram's horn on Rosh ha-Shanah, New Year Day, was attached in the haggadic lore to the ram in Isaac's story.[14]

---

[12] B. Rosh ha-Shanah 10b.

[13] Lev. R. 29:8, Pesikta Kahana 154a.

[14] B. Rosh ha-Shanah 16a. Some interpreted (Gen. 22:14) "Whence the saying today," that it was Rosh ha-Shanah; cf. Pesikta R. 171b; Bereshit Rabbati, p. 91; Neweh Shalom, p. 51. Midrash Aggadah, p. 53: Hence it was said that it was Rosh ha-Shanah when Isaac underwent Akedah. Cf. Abudraham, Rosh ha-Shanah (Warsaw, 1877), 144b: In the midrash it is said that Isaac's Akedah took place on Rosh ha-Shanah. According to others the Akedah took place on Yom Kippur; cf. Ibn Shuaib, at the beginning of the homily for Yom Kippur: The holy tenth day . . . And in the Midrash it is said that then Isaac's Akedah occurred. This season was favored by the Kabbalists;

cf. Menahem of Recanati, Commentary on the Torah, Wa-Yera pericope, and R. Menahem Azariah Fano, Asarah Maamarot, Em Kol Hai, III, 32, that Isaac's Akedah took place on Yom Kippur at the hour of the Minhah service (Zohar, Wa-Yeṣe pericope, 184b: "at twilight"). Cf. R. David Luria's commentary on PRE, ch. 31, nn. 44 and 72, and also what V. Aptowitzer wrote in *Ha-Zofeh le-Hokmat Yisrael*, II, p. 125, n. 3; and, above all, L. Ginzberg, *Commentary on Palestinian Talmud*, III, p. 186ff.: he saw well "that at first they said that the Rosh ha-Shanah shofar suits Isaac's Akedah—hence both these acts took place on Rosh ha-Shanah. And this is the way of the Haggadah, to fit together a number of details if there is some resem-

The fact is, however, that in haggadic lore, the recollection of the Akedah's association with Passover did not vanish. "When the Holy One, blessed be He, chose His world, He also fixed for Himself an order of new moons and years. And when He chose Jacob and his sons, He fixed for Himself the new moon of Redemption, in which Israel were redeemed from Egypt and in which they will be redeemed in the future, as it is said (Mic. 7:15), 'As in the days of thy coming forth out of the land of Egypt, I will yet show unto him marvelous things'; and in this month Isaac was born, and in it he was brought to the Akedah." [15] Now, this is an ancient tradition; we find the like also in the Book of Jubilees. [16] Here it is said that after the incident of the Akedah, Abraham fixed an annual seven-day festival as a memorial of the seven days he spent journeying to the land of Moriah and returning from it in peace. And this became for him and his seed, the children of Israel, an eternal statute, inscribed on the heavenly tables, that in thanksgiving and joy before the Lord they were to keep the days of this festival at the proper time.

In the Haggadah too there survive traces of the connection between the Akedah and the archaic practice of sacrificing human first born: "R. Joshua of Siknin in the name of R. Levi: Although the words themselves refer to Mesha, king of Moab, the verse is in fact speaking of none other than Isaac, when it reads (Mic. 6:6f.), 'Wherewith shall I come before the Lord, and bow myself before God on high. . . . Shall I give *my first born* for my transgression, the fruit of my body for the sin of my soul?' " [17] Thus one learns

blance among them." [See now also S. D. Goitein, *Jewish Education in Muslim Countries Based on Records from the Cairo Genizah* [in Hebrew] (Jerusalem, 1962), pp. 100f.]

[15] Exod. R. 15:11.

[16] 18:18-19. See R. H. Charles, *The Book of Jubilees* (London, 1902), p. 124.

[17] Gen. R. 55:5.

from the prophet's words that already in his time, evidently, idol-worshipers believed that slaying the first born serves as an *atonement* for sin, individual or communal. It is quite likely that there was also an ancient link of association between the ideal of the atonement for all and the sacrifice of the first born, through whose death the whole community is purified and saved. And perhaps this religious notion was already incorporated in the cult of the sacrifice of the First Born in the Spring New Year, and the idol-worshipers, by means of the blood of the first born sacrificed on the threshold of the New Year, wished to be purged of the calamities and curses of the old year.

"The blood of Isaac's Akedah" is quite possibly a survival of ancient legends which once upon a time celebrated and memorialized saving miracles taking place in the month of Nisan, and brought together the Akedah theme with paschal sacrifices, possibly even with the archaic sacrifice of first born. It may be that here are the last and faint echoes of some primitive pagan or prebiblical version of the Akedah story. Possibly too, "the blood of Isaac's Akedah" may be a fossil expression from the world of idolatry, some tiny stone fragment from pagan ruins sunk into the edifice of the talmudic haggadah—and therefore we would have here, as occasionally also elsewhere in the Midrashim of early generations, some leftovers of belief before the beliefs of Israel.

Be that as it may, like the haggadah on "the ashes of Isaac," "the blood of Isaac's Akedah" is carefully preserved, forever to serve as atonement and advocate of Israel in every generation. And whenever Isaac's descendants are in straits, He, as it were, beholds the blood of his Akedah, and pity fills Him so that He turns away the wrath of His anger from His city and His people. This is what we have read in the annals of David's reign, when plague and pestilence broke loose in the Land: " 'And as he was about to destroy, the

Lord beheld, and He repented Him of the evil' (I Chron. 21:15).
What did He behold? He beheld the blood of Isaac's Akedah" [18]
—and immediately His compassion conquers His anger and He
redeems and delivers.

It may well be that "the blood of Isaac's Akedah" surviving in our
sources is nothing other than an archaic cliché, in origin probably a
pagan figure of speech whose pagan soul has left it. And yet, this
relic of an archaic manner of speaking—emptied though it be of its
original idolatrous substance—is a distinct echo of those early times
when the expression was first coined and believed in, literally,
actually. If in the haggadic lore it was possible to pour together the
paschal blood with the blood of Isaac's Akedah, this is a sign that
once upon a time they did imagine that the hand was laid on the lad,
the knife did make contact with the throat, and did what it did
contrary to what is written in the Torah.

In the Haggadah of the talmudic Sages the attempt to defy Scripture and ignore its signals was made and succeeded. Or perhaps the
Haggadah recovered for Judaism something of that legacy the
Torah wished to renounce, or at least to subdue. Out of its longing
to provide atonement for the sins of Israel (N.B. "there is no atonement without blood!" [19]) the Haggadah brought to completion the
deed of the father, the first in a long line of those who were to
bind for the altar, and made full the righteous piety of the son, the
first in a long line of those who were to be bound on an altar; and
of the blood of the Akedah made an offering on high where it might
serve as protection and guardian of Israel until the end comes nigh.

Again, therefore, what do we find? That it was not in the Middle
Ages that this haggadah was invented. Passover and Akedah go hand

[18] See above, n. 1.
[19] B. Yoma 5a, B. Zebahim 6a, B. Menahot 93b.

in hand on the New Year of the ancient calendar and festival of the first born in the pastoral society of antiquity. Who knows? Maybe in the blood of Isaac's Akedah, as in his sacrifice in the first month of spring, there is a speck of a hint that the roots of that haggadah on the slaughter of Isaac reach back to a remote past of the world of idolatry, possibly before biblical religion came into being.

VIII

*"And Abraham called the name of the place,
May the Lord Regard" (Gen. 22:14) — May God regard
this as though I slaughtered my son before Thee.*[1]

If Isaac was sacrificed for a sweet savor to the Lord, what can these
verses possibly mean: "And behold a ram after" and so on? "And
he offered it as a burnt offering *in place of* his son"?

What does midrashic exegesis suggest? "What is the meaning of
'after' (*aḥar*) (Gen. 22:13)? After all that happened."[2] "(The
ram appeared) after everything was done in connection with Isaac's
Akedah."[3] "So Abraham went and took the ram and offered it up
as a burnt offering." Surely nothing else is wanting in the verse.
What need then to add " '*taḥat* his son'? Said the Holy One,
blessed be He, By your life! First your son was the one sacrificed,
but now this ram too, after that."[4] In other words, Abraham
offered up two sacrifices, he began with the sacrifice of the son
and ended with the sacrifice of the ram.

The commentators found support in Scripture. In the Hebrew
language, the word *taḥat* has two connotations, one spatial and the

---

[1] Midrash Aggadah, ed. S. Buber, p. 53.

[2] Gen. R. 56:9, with which clause, however, the commentators have considerable difficulty; cf. Yefeh Toar *ad* Gen. R., loc. cit., and Theodor, p. 605. See M. M.

Kasher, *Torah Shelemah*, p. 901, #148. Note the interpretation in Sekel Tob, p. 62.

[3] MhG, p. 356.

[4] Tanhuma, Shelah, 14.

other temporal. Hence *"tahat* his son" (Gen. 22:13) may mean
either *in place of* or *after* his son. And both these meanings are furnished in the name of R. Benaiah, among the last of the Tannaim.
In R. Benaiah's name, R. Pinhas taught one approach: " 'And he
offered it up as a burnt offering *tahat* his son'—he said to Him:
Master of the whole universe, do Thou regard (what I have done)
as though first I sacrificed my son Isaac and thereafter I sacrificed
this ram, *tahat,* after, him; as one says (II Kings 15:7), 'And Azariah
slept with his fathers . . . and Jotham his son reigned *tahat* him,'
in his stead," [5] where the meaning must be *after* him.

Also in the name of R. Benaiah, R. Yudan presented another approach in the interpretation of *"tahat* his son." [6] Abraham said
before Him: Master of the whole universe, behold, I am slaughtering the ram; do Thou regard this as though my son Isaac is slain before Thee. He took the blood of the ram and said: Do Thou regard
this as though the blood of my son were being poured before Thee.
As Abraham skinned the ram, he said: Do Thou regard this as
though it were the skin of my son Isaac which is being flayed before
Thee. As he coated the ram with salt, [7] he said: Do Thou regard
this as though the salt were being poured on my son Isaac. As he
offered the limbs of the ram, he said: Do Thou regard this as
though these were the limbs of my son Isaac being offered to Thee.
As he burned the ram, he said: Do Thou regard this as though the
ashes of my son Isaac were heaped up on top of the altar before
Thee. So, during each and every step of the sacrificial service, as
he did something to the ram, he would say: Do Thou regard this
as though it were being done to my son Isaac—quite like the ancient

---

[5] Gen. R. 56:9.
[6] Gen. R., *ad* Gen. 22:13; Tanhuma, loc.
cit. (Shelah, 14); Num. R. 17:2; Pesikta
R., 40, 171a; Yalkut #101 (end); Midrash Aggadah, p. 53; Sefer ha-Yashar, p.
81; Rashi and R. Bahya *ad loc.*
[7] See M. Zebahim 6:5.

formula: (If one says,) Now, this for that, this in place of that, this in exchange of that, the substitution is valid.[8]

Echoes of an archaic rite rise from between the lines of this midrash. The fact is that R. Benaiah can be supported by rites of sacrifice that are preserved in Canaanite inscriptions. In North Africa, in Algeria, in the neighborhood of N'gaous (called Nicivibus by the Romans), three votive stelae from the end of the second or beginning of the third century—in other words, in the very age of R. Benaiah—were discovered among the ruins of an ancient sanctuary dedicated to Saturn (equals Sabbathai!). On these stelae is engraved the god's image; he is pictured holding a knife in his right hand, and before him squats a ram—as in the Akedah story. Under the representation is a Latin inscription telling that So-and-So and So-and-So, man and wife, wish to be remembered and inscribed for welfare, because they had carried out what in a night vision[9] they were commanded to do, or what they vowed[10] to do, and offered up as a burnt offering a lamb in place of [the first born of?] their children. Now, although in this Roman province Canaanite ceased to be a spoken language, in the religion alive in that region Canaanite terms and beliefs persisted, and in the Latin inscription just referred to, the sacrifice mentioned above is called by a name which has survived from the Punic and occurs in Punic inscriptions —*molchomor* or *morchomor*, that is, *mlk'amr*, to wit, a lamb sacrifice.[11]

In theory, the demands of the primitive religion were never forgotten: every first issue of the womb is sacred to the gods, and even

[8] M. Temurah 5:5.

[9] *ex viso,* cf. D. Kimhi *ad* Gen. 22:3 (cited above, ch. I, n. 11).

[10] *ex voto.*

[11] J. Carcopino, in *Revue de l'histoire des*

religions, CVI (1932), 592ff.; A. Atl, *ZAW,* LII (1934), 305ff.; O. Eissfeldt, *Molk als Opferbegriff im Punischen und Hebräischen* (Halle, 1935); N. H. Torczyner, *Ha-Lashon we-ha-Sefer* (Jerusalem, 1948), I, p. 72.

the human first born is theirs by right. Nevertheless, for practical purposes, the celestial ones are prepared to be satisfied with a substitution for the human offering, a lamb sacrifice. As is to be seen from the inscriptions, the votary of a *mlk'amr* would recite before the god as follows: *A soul for a soul, blood for blood, life for life, let the lamb come as vicarious offering.*[13] We can see from here where this idiom was born: its origin derives from the archaic religion, its primary setting is in the sacrificial cult and not in criminal or civil law. Such formulae are liturgical accompaniments recited when proxy offerings take place. The style of such prayers is a combination of proclamation and solemn supplication, intended to appease, and to beseech the deity that he regard and accept the substitution with favor: the soul of the lamb for the soul of the man, the blood of the lamb for the blood of the man, the life of the lamb for the life of the man. Thus on offering each single part of the lamb the man recites: May this appear before the god as though it were my son that I offered, this for that, an eye for an eye, tooth for tooth, hand for hand, foot for foot.

Note well the language R. Benaiah uses—for in it survives something of the beliefs and practices of a twilight generation, when the old and new are in a confusion. The legacy of the ancients has not yet been entirely forgotten: the ancients can accept the rigors of sacrifice as they offer up their own first born to the gods, because they have not yet discovered mercy's function within justice. It is only inch by inch that law and statute were mellowed and humanized and that, in sacrifices, the descendants of the ancients learned to substitute an animal for the human.

It may well be that in the narrative of the ram which Abraham sacrificed as a burnt offering in place of his son, there is historical

---

[13] *anima pro anima, sanguine pro sanguine, vita pro vita . . . agnum pro vikario.*

remembrance of the transition to animal sacrifice from human sacrifice—a religious and moral achievement which in the folk memory was associated with Abraham's name, the father of the new faith and the first of the upright in the Lord's way. And quite possibly the primary purpose of the Akedah story may have been only this: to attach to a real pillar of the folk and a revered reputation the new norm—abolish human sacrifice, substitute animals instead.

In truth, this was a daring innovation and was not at once accepted. For a long time people were in a quandary, especially in moments of distress—perhaps after all the ancient law was the right one? In times of crisis, in the midst of danger, there were always those who slipped back and once more carried out to the letter the sacrifice of children. Over a long stretch of time parental love engaged in battle with the fear of the gods, the quality of mercy with the quality of mercilessness. And, as usual, what man sought was both ends of the rope, holding on to one end while not letting the other go. He was being drawn gradually to the notion of animal sacrifice, but he strained every muscle to retain at least something of the old ways.

As in the Haggadah of the talmudic Sages: When Abraham had been forbidden to lay hand on Isaac, he said: Let me extract from him one drop of blood and let this be regarded as though I had slaughtered him.[13] You will indeed find such compromises in the pagan world—for death they substituted a little physical suffering: a slight incision would be made in a man's neck, a few drops of blood were let fall, and after this token wounding the victim would be set free.[14] In the distant past it was the practice in Sparta to sacrifice a human being and to sprinkle his blood on the altar. There was a tradition in their possession that the gods had com-

---

[13] Gen. R. 56:7 and Midrash Aggadah, p. 53. [14] Euripides, *Jphig. in Taur.* 1450 sqq.

manded that human blood be shed on their altar. Finally Lycurgus ordered that instead young boys be flogged; henceforth with their blood the altar would be dampened.[15] Some did what they could to disguise facts and to hide from the gods the very substitution of beast for man. There was the instance of the Greek father who volunteered to sacrifice his daughter to the goddess Artemis, in order to put an end to the plague which had swept the country. On the day of the sacrifice he brought a she-goat covered in the girl's dress, and sacrificed the animal in place of his daughter.[16] We find something similar in connection with the god Dionysus, "devourer of men": calves of the stall were treated as though they were favorite children; on their hooves baby shoes were tied; and in every respect the votaries behaved as though it was their children they were bringing forth to slaughter.[17]

Now although of course it is out of the question for such pagan notions and ways to be preserved in rabbinic literature, remnants of something similar do indeed survive in the kind of exegesis we have already referred to, for example, that bellwether ram of Abraham's flock, called Isaac: "Said the Holy One, blessed be He, Let *Isaac for Isaac* come!"[18] Right down to the present a touch of the archaic patterns of thinking survives, in the ceremony known as *Kapparot*. In some districts they would use for this ceremony "proxy rams, or any creature with horns, reminiscent of Isaac's ram."[19] Since, however, cattle are rather costly, for the most part it became customary to use a rooster as the substitute sacrifice—for

[15] Pausanias 3.16, 10.

[16] Eustathius, *Commentarii ad Homeri Iliadem* 2.732 (Leipzig, 1825, p. 331).

[17] Aelian, *De natura animalium* 12.34.

[18] See above, ch. V, n. 12.

[19] Responsum of Mar Rav Sheshna, a Sura Gaon, in *Shaare Teshuvah*, #229 = Tur, Orah Hayyim, sec. 605. Cf. V. Aptowitzer, in *Ha-Zofeh le-Hokmat Yisrael*, VII, p. 93; J. Z. Lauterbach, "The Ritual for the Kapparot Ceremony," *Jewish Studies in Memory of George A. Kohut* (New York, 1935), p. 419; idem, "Tashlik," *HUCA*, XI (1936), 262ff.

the Hebrew for "rooster" is *gever*, and *gever* is also "man";[20] with
a sleight of wit, the distinction between man and his proxy loses all
reality: *Let gever for gever come!* Let the bird to death withdraw,
and let the quondam sinner enter life and all felicity! Leading rabbinic authorities railed against the Kapparot ceremony. In vain. They
did everything they could to put an end to this way of the Amor-
ites.[21] The ceremony retained its hold[22] on the people at large, they
loved it—no wonder, for it feeds on a heritage from the remote past.

In R. Benaiah's midrash also, trustworthy recollections of the
ancient ways are preserved, and, as already said, its idiom makes it
possible for us to appreciate the profound revolution in the history
of religion, when the primitive blood sacrifice was abolished. The
force of the primitive ways had not yet been forgotten, the heart
had not yet abandoned the notion of the sanctity of the human first
born. And when a man sacrificed his beast rather than his first born,
he acted and spoke the way Abraham did in this haggadah, as he
was sacrificing the ram: "Now as he bound it, and slaughtered it,
and burned it, he kept saying: That in place of my son, and that in
place of my son, and that in place of my son!"[23] And what is more,
this midrash has something to it which perhaps may help us approach the meaning and principal intent of the biblical Akedah
story.

Bible critics disagree. Some believe that the mention of the land
of Moriah and the mountain of the Lord occurred already in the
original Akedah narrative. Some believe that these details were added

[20] What is the meaning of the call of the *gever?* Rab said: *Man (gavra)* has called. In Rab Shila's school they said: The *cock* has crowed.—B. Yoma 20a. Cf. J. Sukkah 5:5, 55c = J. Shekalim 5:2, 48d.

[21] Nahmanides and Rashba (Orhot Hay-yim, Hilkot Erev Yom Kippur), Bet Yosef (cf. Shulhan Aruk, Orah Hayyim, sec.

605; in first edition: "it's a foolish cus-tom") and Hezekia da Silva, Peri Hadash. Cf. R. Zevi Chajes, *Darke Horaah* (Zol-kiev, 1842), 9b.

[22] Cf. Isserles, Orah Hayyim, sec. 605.

[23] Midrash Akedat Yizhak; cf. M. Higger, *Halakot we-Aggadot* (New York, 1933), p. 72.

at a later date, in order to exalt and proclaim the lineage of the Temple in Jerusalem. In his habitual way, Abraham ibn Ezra[24] drops hints: "If you will use your wits, etc., 'On the mountain of the Lord there will appear,' etc., you will recognize the truth." No different is also the interpretation, in the volume *Sekel Job,*[25] by his innocent-minded contemporary: " 'On the mountain of the Lord, *there will appear,'* cf. the idiom (Deut. 16:16), 'All your males *shall appear.'* " And so too the comment in *Midrash ha-Gadol:*[26] " 'Whence the present saying' etc. (Gen. 22:15)—Scripture teaches that already Father Abraham knew that this was to be the site of the Temple-service for all generations." The fact is, considering the rabbinic approach, there was no difficulty with such exegesis, since Abraham was privy even to the new name the Holy One, blessed be He, was going to give to Jerusalem in the future.[27]

In the Akedah version as we have it now, it is difficult not to feel deliberate conjunction of (seven, more likely, five) wordplays: Moriah [*wa-yar'*, and he saw the place], God *yir'eh lo,* will see to, *yere' elohim* (God-fearing) [*wa-yar'*, and he saw, and behold, a ram], the Lord *yir'eh* (will see), on the mount the Lord *yera'eh* (will be seen). These are stylistic devices of narrative, and possibly also signs of the language of antiquity. This is also one of Scripture's ways to emphasize or underscore its principal intentions. It has been well said that *Adonai-yireh* (the Lord will see to) is a name based on what had taken place: "God will *see* to (*yir'eh lo*) the sheep for His burnt offering." [28] Abraham prophesied not knowing that he was uttering a prophecy; for when he uttered those words, his only pur-

---

[24] In his commentary *ad* Deut. 1:9.

[25] P. 63, and so too Lekah Tob, p. 101: On the basis of the idiom of "all your males shall appear" (Deut. 16:16); hence, "on the mountain of the Lord will appear."

[26] *Ad* Gen. 22:14, p. 358.

[27] Gen. R. 49:2 and 64:4.

[28] Cf. Sekel Tob, p. 63: So according to the *peshat, the literal interpretation*—the reason the Lord named it Adonai-Yireh, the Lord will see, because Isaac

pose at the time was to put Isaac off. But speech is also under covenant, and while the preparations of the heart may be man's, what the tongue expresses is from the Lord.[29] Wherefore the Holy One, blessed be He, answered him, "And he saw, behold, a ram." [30] And because He responded to Abraham on Mount Moriah and Isaac was redeemed,[31] for there by God's will they were provided with a living creature as a sacrifice in place of the son,[32] Abraham called the place by the name *Adonai-yireh*, that is to say, the Lord will see to the substitute for His offering, He will find the appropriate ransom—as if to say, This is the place destined for salvation and here the Lord in His graciousness will make Himself available to those who call upon Him. And if "On the mount of the Lord will be seen" was once a popular saying,[33] then possibly the clause may also be explained as "On the mount the Lord will see to" the ransom of His choice or substitute gift, along the lines of Jephthah's vow: Whatsoever (living creature) cometh forth and is the first thing you chance upon on the Mount of the Lord, that you shall set aside as a (substitute) offering.[34] If that be the case, then perhaps the whole Akedah composition came into being with no purpose other than to teach the lesson and provide the basis for the practice of making

---

had been told, *The Lord will see to* the sheep. So too S. D. Luzatto, *Bikkure ha-Ittim* (1828), p. 151. Wellhausen also felt this: *Die Composition des Hexateuchs*[3] (Berlin, 1899), p. 18.

[29] Prov. 16:1; Cf. B. Moed Katan 18a, and Tanhuma, ed. Buber, Wa-Yera, 46, p. 113.

[30] Cf. Midrashe Teman cited in M. M. Kasher, *Torah Shelemah*, p. 884, #97.

[31] M. Taanit 2:4; cf. Jerushalmi *ad loc.*, 65d. And cf. Derek Emet, Zohar, I, 120b: God answered Abraham on Mount Moriah by providing him with a ram.

[32] Cf. R. Samuel ben Meir and Obadiah Sforno *ad* Gen. 22:13.

[33] "Hence the saying today"—cf. Gen. 10:9, I Sam. 10:12 and 19:24.

[34] Judg. 11:31. See Gen. R. 64:19: "Because the Lord your God granted me good fortune" (Gen. 27:20)—R. Johanan and Resh Lakish: One of them said, If He made provision for your sacrifice, as it is written (Gen. 22:13), And he looked, and behold, a ram, all the more for your nourishment! The other said, If He made provision for you to have a life's mate, as it is written (24:63), And he looked, and behold, camels approaching, all the more for your nourishment.

proxy offerings. In this way the talmudic Sages in fact sought to explain the place name itself. What is the meaning of Moriah? *Temurah*, a substitute offering, an exchange, as in the idiom of "One may not exchange or substitute, *yamir*, for it" (Lev. 27:10).[85]

But why these wordplays on *ra'ah* and *wa-yar'* anyway? Perhaps in this fashion to hint at and explain the meaning of one of the most ancient terms for sanctuary and altar, *Arel* (Ariel) or *Harel*, which entered Hebrew speech from the language and culture of the ancient Sumerians.[86] In Hebrew speech such names almost spontaneously attach themselves to the sounds of *re'iyyah, yire'ah,* the vocabulary for "seeing" and "fear": On Mount El, on Harel and Ariel, there El will come into view of those whose fear of Him is true, sure He will see to their salvation—such and other expressions sung in praise of Jerusalem.

This may be said then: In the biblical account of the Akedah the legend of the *name of the place* was amalgamated with the legend on *the institution of substitutes* in sacrifice. In the latter, the expression "Adonai-yireh," and possibly also "On the mount of the Lord He will be seen," were related to what happened to Abraham, that the Lord saw to it that he would have a living creature to offer in place of his son; and thus He prevented the fruit of the Patriarch's body from falling into the pit. The Lord did not violate His covenant with Abraham and did not retreat from what He had vouchsafed, to fulfill the promise that "it is through Isaac that offspring shall be continued for you."[87] Therefore Abraham made known

[85] Pesikta R., 40: so read R. Ephraim Zalman Margoliot; cf. the commentary *Zera' Ephraim* in Pesikta R. (Warsaw, 1893). On the other hand, cf. the comment of M. Friedmann, Pesikta R. 170a, citing Yalkut, Canticles, #988: Moriah, Temurah (substitute, proxy)—Abraham became a high priest in place of Shem ben Noah. So too in Bereshit Rabbati, p. 86.

[86] Sum. *arali.*, Acc. *arallu:* cf. Knut Tallquist, *Sumerisch-akkadische Namen der Totenwelt*, in *Studia Orientalia* (Helsinki, 1934), V, pp. 6f.; W. F. Albright, *JBL*, XXXIX (1920), p. 137; idem, *Archaeology and the Religion of Israel* (1942), pp. 151, 218.

[87] Gen. 21:12; cf. Tanhuma, ed. Buber, Wa-Yera, 40.

and proclaimed throughout the world true fear of the Lord, and he commanded his sons and his household after him to make proxy sacrifices, that is, animal sacrifice in place of human.

On the other hand, in the legend about the place name, the original signification of "Adonai-yireh" and "On the mount of the Lord He will be seen" was so broadened as to include all the praises of Jerusalem and all the glories of that place "where Mine eyes and My heart shall be perpetually." [38] It is even possible that on the lips of the pilgrims, who are wont to sing the praises of their sanctuary as they make the festival pilgrimage, the very name "Adonai-yireh" became a kind of formula for the whole aggregate of salvations and hopes attached to Him who dwells on Mount Zion. There the Lord commanded the blessing, even life forever; there they that seek the Lord are not in want of any good thing; there all the righteous are delivered out of trouble. If a person was rash and made a vow or took an oath, or got himself inextricably entangled in sin, there *the Lord will see to* his relief and deliverance, by providing him with some substitute or ransom, to atone for his error or folly. Therefore, if anything is too baffling for you, or you have no idea whence help comes, up and get you to the Mount of El: On Moriah's peak, Yah will be found by those who seek, and you will hear for Yah will speak; from here He will cause His countenance to shine on thee, and in His light, light thou shalt see. This is why it became proverbial that *whatever* the want and whatever the need of *every* living being in *the Mount of the Lord*, it will be seen to. There will be found the balm for everyone heartsick and the joy for every grief. All the fountains of salvation are there.

The legend about the institution of proxy sacrifice and the legend on Moriah's praises came together to proclaim not merely the per-

---

[38] I Kings 9:3.

missibility but superiority of the new pattern in gifts to God. Both these legends proceed to announce that henceforth if anyone wishes to take upon himself the strict obligation of ancient practice to sacrifice the first issue of the human womb, not only is this not a sign of extra piety or scrupulous observance, it is downright sin and profaning of the Name of Heaven. As for him who seemingly adopts the easier way, in that he withholds his child from the altar, let him feel no compunctions about the matter out of fear that he has failed to meet his obligations to offer up a living creature. The very reverse! In such conduct lies his excellence, he is the one who has offered up what is choicest. Fortunate indeed is the one who offered up on Mount Moriah proxy sacrifices! Him the First Fathers' righteousness upholds, and the merit of this holy place—which is the place where the wood was laid, the Binding was made, and the oath not to be betrayed was sworn; this is the mountain which God hath desired for His abode and the House He longed for as the place to put His Name forever. It is here displeasing to the Lord when you give your first born for your transgression and the fruit of your body for the sin of your soul. It is quite enough for you to lay your hand upon the head of the (animal) burnt offering, and that will be acceptable in your behalf, in expiation for you. The name of this place is *Adonai-yireh*, for the Omnipresent will regard it as though you slew your son before Him. What, still in doubt? Look now to the Rock from which you were hewn, to the Father of your folk and your faith: "Had God asked Father Abraham for his eyeball, he would have plucked it out and given it to Him. And not just his eyeball—he would have given Him his very soul, which was the most precious of all to him. For it is said, 'Take now your son, your favored one, Isaac, whom you love.' Well then, is not Isaac specifically mentioned? What point is there to 'your favored one'? That (however) is a reference to Abraham's soul, for the soul is called 'favored one,' as it is said, 'Deliver my soul from the sword, my favorite from the power of the dog' " (Ps. 22:21).[39] Talk of the extent of fear of Heaven! And yet! "Don't you lay your hand." "And don't you do anything." You're looking for supererogatory acts? Stop looking.

Perhaps here also are the beginnings of the idea of *the Merit of the Akedah*, which at first may have come simply to ornament the *site of the Akedah* and was intended to be no more than one of the glories of Mount Moriah. Depend on it, the Temple Mount has been singled out for grace and mercy and compassion. Accompanying every one of the sacrifices being offered *in this place* is the memory and good work of the one who came to bind and the one who came to be bound. Thus the merit of the Akedah endures forever, and is cherished and recalled before the Lord at each burnt offering and sacrifice presented on this choicest of all locations.[40]

Here it would be unimaginable—it would never even occur to one—that God requires or delights in human sacrifice. On Mount Moriah, taught Havayah, not human—animal sacrifice I require! Here were laid the foundation and cornerstone for the entire complex of divine service on the Temple Mount—human sacrifice, *forbidden*, substitution of another living creature for the human, *per-*

[39] Sifre Deut., 313; Tanhuma, Shelah, 14, ed. Buber, 27, IV, p. 72; Num. R. 17 and Pesikta R. 171a.

[40] That was fine feeling on the part of Nahmanides (in his commentary *ad* Gen. 22:2) that this was one of the principal intentions of the Akedah chapter: "And He commanded him to offer up (the lad) *in that place* . . . and what he wanted was that *the Akedah Merit persist forever in the sacrifices*, as Abraham said, *The Lord will see to.*" Cf. Bereshit Rabbati, p. 91: "*In the mountain of the Lord will*

be seen, the Akedah which was enacted long ago, O Lord, *let it be beheld before Thee* for generations to come." And see the commentary of R. Joseph Bekor Shor (ed. A. Jellinek, Leipzig, 1856, pp. 33ff.): "*Adonai-yireh*, that is to say, Let the Omnipresent behold and remember the performance." Perhaps therefore the meaning might be: *Adonai-yireh, Let the Lord take note* of everything that was done to Isaac *in this place*, and add his merit to every sacrifice which will be offered here generation after generation.

mitted. And one may regard the biblical Akedah story as a kind of confirmation from Heaven and approval by the Most High, of the rightness, the propriety of the Temple-service in Jerusalem.

The biblical account, then, came to enforce and validate a new way of worship; and, too, it came to abolish and discredit the statutes of the ancient world. The Akedah story repels once for all the primitive notion of the sanctity of the human first born and its derivative demand for the literal sacrifice of children. The Akedah story declared war on *the remnants of idolatry in Israel* and undertook to remove root and branch the whole long, terror-laden inheritance from idolatrous generations.

In this attack on the survivals of alien creeds Scripture and Midrash were at one. The haggadic lore of the talmudic Sages continued battling along these lines and under such standards, against every vestige of an idolatrous heritage—be it ever so popular or sanctified in human eyes—and knew no peace until it had either eliminated it from Judaism or explained it away. Note well how the Rabbis labored to remove from its literal meaning any trace of the pagan inheritance. The verse reads (Lev. 1:11), "It shall be slaughtered before the Lord *on the north* (*safonah*) side of the altar." In order to wipe out every footprint of idolatry's cult which fixed the seat of the gods "upon the mount of meeting, in the uttermost parts of the north" (Isa. 14:13), the Rabbis were not at all timid about deriving the word "*safonah*" (on the north) from the root *sfn*, which signifies laying-up and safekeeping, as in "New and old which I have laid up, *safanti*, for thee, O my beloved" (Cant. 7:14); even in that verse they found support and reminiscence of *the Akedah Merit* which is put into permanent safekeeping and is *laid up* (*sefunah*) *before the Lord:* "The very day that Father Abraham put up his son Isaac on top of the altar, the Holy One, blessed be He, instituted (the Tamid, Perpetual, offerings of) the two lambs, the one for morning and the one for twilight. And to what end? So that at the hour when Israel offer up the Tamid on the altar and recite this verse, 'ṣafonah before the Lord,' the Holy One, blessed be He, might recall the Akedah of Isaac son of Abraham. I summon heaven and earth as my witnesses! When Gentile or Jew, man or woman, male or female slave, recite this verse, 'ṣafonah before the Lord,' the Holy One, blessed be He, recalls the Akedah of Isaac ben Abraham." [41]

And the Rabbis did the same with the practice of the Rosh ha-Shanah Shofar ceremony, the sounding of the ram's horn on the New Year. There is doubtless an ancient idolatrous basis for the rite of sounding horns and trumpetings in sanctuaries at the beginning of new moons. It may well be that in earliest times the beginning of the first month, that is, Rosh ha-Shanah, the beginning of the year, was distinguished from the remaining months only by this, that on it extra blasts were sounded. "The roots of sounding the horn go back to primitive practice in moon worship, and the purpose of such sound is to drive off the forces of evil that rise against the new moon on the night of its first appearance." [49] Sound and fury [43] with horns when the moon's face is covered come to

---

[41] Seder Eliyahu R., 7, ed. Friedmann, p. 36—Lev. R. 2 — Yalkut, #99.

[49] Yehezkel Kaufmann, *Toledot ha-Emunah ha-Yisraelit*, II, part 5, p. 492. A vague recollection of the ancient myth survived in the Kabbalah; cf., for example, Zohar, Raya Mehemna, Emor pericope, III, 98b ff.: "That day on which the moon is covered up and the world stands on trial, that accuser *covers up and curtains off from view* and locks the doorway to the King . . . ; and on that day he is granted leave to *cover up* the doorway to the King, and *the moon is put out of view* until sentence is passed on all the inhabitants of the world."

[43] Jer. 20:16: "A cry in the morning, and

an alarm at noontide." A day when the alarm (is sounded) (Num. 29:1), Aramaic version, A day of sobs; cf. B. Rosh ha-Shanah 33b: "And it is written *of Sisera's mother* (Judg. 5:28), Sob did the mother of Sisera." The practice of sounding from the shofar one hundred notes on Rosh ha-Shanah, to correspond to the one hundred outcries which *Sisera's mother* cried out, is cited in the works of the early rabbinic authorities, as on the authority of "the Jerushalmi" (Aruch, s.v. '*rb;* R. Hananel's commentary, end of the treatise B. Rosh ha-Shanah; Tosafot *ad* B. Rosh ha-Shanah 33b, s.v. *shi'ur teruah;* Pardes, ed. Ehrenreich, p. 219; Ha-Manhig, Rosh ha-Shanah, 21, Berlin,

terrify the demons, lest because of them the full moon be delayed and fail to be restored. But Scripture already gave to the practice of sounding the horn a fundamentally new explanation which liber-

---

1856, 54b, who found some support for this in Yelamdenu, Emor pericope [= Tanhuma, Emor, 11, Tazria, 4, Lev. R. 27:7, and Pesikta Kahana 77b]: "Ye are nothing, and your work *of a quality to cry out over (me-'apa')*" (Isa. 41:24) — by *notarikon* the expression is interpreted as, *of one hundred outcries (mi-me'ah pe'iyyot)* which a woman cries out when she is on the birthstool, ninety-nine of which make you think of death and only one of which makes you think of life; Rabiah, Rosh ha-Shanah, 541, II, p. 238; Shibbole ha-Leket, end of sec. 301; Or Zarua, Rosh ha-Shanah, sec. 269, end). The late Benjamin Lewin, in Kontros 'Irbub ha-Satan (in *Ha-Tor*, 1926; republished later in *Ozar ha-Geonim*, V, 89-93), tried to explain that the reference to "Jerushalmi" was a mistaken caption for a Midrash on a vision of *Jerusalem* of the Future. See his interesting comment, but the matter requires further thought.

Some tried to judaize the allusion to Canaanite customs; see J. Reifman, *Ha-Zefirah*, I (1874), 78 (and see also the annual *Ha-Carmel*, I, 553, and Or *Torah*, 205), who emended the text to read: "the one hundred outcries which *Mother Sarah* cried out." So too Ratner, *Ahabat Zion Wirushalayim ad* Rosh ha-Shanah, p. 57; and both of them called attention to the Midrash cited by Abudraham, Rosh ha-Shanah (Warsaw, 1877), 144b, "that on Rosh ha-Shanah Isaac was bound on the altar, and that day *Mother Sarah* heard of it, and she cried out and sobbed and wailed. That is why the verse says, 'A

day of alarm it shall be for you' (Num. 29:1), which is translated in the Aramaic version as, A day of sobs—the purpose being that the Holy One, blessed be He, shall remember for our sake the wailings of *Mother Sarah*, and forgive us." See also Ginzberg in *Ha-Zofeh*, III, 187 (and cf. his *Legends*, VI, 199, n. 89), that already in Lev. R. 20:2 it is stated that the shofar sounds on Rosh ha-Shanah are in remembrance of Sarah's weeping: "She shrieked 6 times, corresponding to the 6 *teki'ot* (shofar blasts)." Cf. Midrash Zuta *ad* Eccl. 9:7, ed. Buber, p. 121: "She shrieked 6 times, Woe, Woe, corresponding to the 6 *teki'ot*"; PRE, ch. 32: "She wept 3 times, corresponding to 3 *teki'ot*, wailed 3 times corresponding to 3 sobs" (the shofar is made to produce: see M. Rosh ha-Shanah 4:9) (cf. R. David Luria, PRE, loc. cit., n. 15); and Midrash Aggadah, ed. Buber, p. 55: "The reason alarms, *teru'ot*, are sounded on Rosh ha-Shanah is this, that *the death of Sarah may serve as atonement* for them, because *teru'ah* is a groaning and a wailing." Cf. also Bereshit Rabbati, p. 94.

Perhaps this business of *teru'ah*, alarm, and sobs, is much much older even than Sisera's mother, as is evident from the very word *shofar*, itself inherited from the language—and no doubt also from the practice—of the ancient Sumerians: Sum. *šeg-bar*: cf. B. Landsberger, *Die Fauna des alten Mesopotamien* (Leipzig, 1934), pp. 97f.: "eine später ausgestorbene Wildschaf-spezies, vielleicht *das Tahr.*"

ated the ceremony completely from the world of idolatry and the ritual of expulsion of evil spirits. According to the Torah, what is the reason for sounding the horn at the new moon? "They shall be a *reminder* of you before your God" (Num. 10:10). In this path of biblical religion, in its spirit and image, the talmudic Sages continued when they tied Rosh ha-Shanah to the folk's sacred memories. "Said R. Abbahu: Why is a ram's horn used for the trumpeting? So that I might recall for your sake the Akedah of Isaac son of Abraham, and account it to your credit *as though* you bound yourselves on the altar before Me." [44]

[44] B. Rosh ha-Shanah 16a. On the subject of R. Abbahu's regulation in regard to the shofar service, cf. B. Rosh ha-Shanah 34a and R. Hai Gaon's Responsum, *Ozar ha-Geonim*, Rosh ha-Shanah, pp. 60ff.

IX

*"And Abraham took the wood
for the burnt offering, and put
it on his son Isaac" (Gen. 22:6) —
like one bearing his own cross.*[1]

In Scripture, then, the Akedah triumphed, and in the Torah gave no foothold to any pagan, prebiblical notion of slaying and sending up the son in smoke. Had the Akedah succeeded likewise in life and in the realities of history, not a trace of heathen legend or lore on this theme would have survived in Judaism. But since traces did remain, age-old beliefs continued to nest in the thickets of the soul. It is very hard to drive out pagan spirits, and each generation must renew the battle against them. What is more, the very measures adopted to expel them are frequently themselves a partial admission of the vitality of pagan ways. You will even find that the ones who battle against the nightmare of human sacrifice of the first born are themselves not liberated from the power of the ancient demand— there is still a willing ear and a ready tongue for images and words out of the province of archaic belief: Do Thou regard it *as though* I had first offered up my son Isaac.[2] Do Thou regard it *as though* Isaac's blood is being poured out before Thee, and so on: *as though* his ashes were heaped up before Thee.[3] *Adonai-yireh,*

[1] Gen. R. 56:3. Cf. Pesikta R., ch. 31, 143b; Yalkut, #101; Yelamdenu in Yalkut Talmud Torah, Mann, p. 308.

[2] Gen. R. 56:9.
[3] Tanhuma, Shelah, 14.

may God take note of it that it is *as though* I have slain my son before Thee.[4] I account it to you *as though* you offered yourselves on the altar before Me.[5] And many more such. And the idolatrous impulse whispers and murmurs its black logic in the ear: If on high the mere *as though* is so highly regarded, imagine the power of *the actual!* And every mother's son submits with a sigh: If only we could convert this *as though* and get it down and get it done on the altar, imagine the increase of grace from before Him!

So that impulse prods—and contact with the alien environment performs even more. Search and you shall find the signs in our literature.

"The villain Balaam was the *synagoros*, the advocate, of the Nations of the World, and he said: 'Will the Lord be pleased with thousands of rams, with ten thousands of rivers of oil? (Mic. 6:7)' Is He so pleased with the one *log* of oil you offer Him? We will offer Him myriads upon myriads of oil streams! What is it that Abraham offered up before Him? One ram, was it not? As it is said, 'And behold, *one* ram' (Gen. 22:13).[6] If He wishes, we will offer up to Him thousands of rams. What indeed did Abraham offer up to Him? His son. I will offer up to Him my son and my daughter, as it is said, 'Lo, I shall give my first born for my transgression' (Mic. 6:7), that is, my first born, my son; 'the fruit of my body for the sin of my soul' (ibid.), that is, my daughter."[7]

Others interpreted[8] the words of this Micah verse as what *Mesha* king of Moab said. What did he do? He assembled all his astrologers and said to them: What is it about this nation that for them such miracles are performed?[9] Why is it that I wage war with many

[4] Midrash Aggadah, p. 53.
[5] B. Rosh ha-Shanah 16a.
[6] And so too in the Aramaic versions.
[7] Tanhuma, ed. Buber, beginning of Saw pericope (III, p. 12), Yalkut, Saw, beginning (#479) Yalkut, Micah, #555.
[8] R. Joshua (of Siknin) in the name of R. Levi, Gen. R. 55:5.
[9] Rashi *ad* II Kings 3:27.

nations and defeat them; but these Jews, they defeat me. Said the astrologers to him: It is all by merit of one elder they had, whose name was Abraham. When he was one hundred years old he was granted an only son; yet the father offered him up (to God). Said Mesha to them: *Did he actually carry that out?* They said to Mesha: *No.* Said he to them: If miracles were performed for his sake though he did not actually carry it out, imagine the consequences if he had carried it out![10] Well now, I too have a first-born son who is to succeed me on the throne. I am going to offer him up and maybe miracles will be performed for our sake, as it is written, "Then he took his first-born son that should have reigned in his stead, and offered him for a burnt offering upon the wall" (II Kings 3:27).

To be sure, the talmudic Sages never wearied of repeating once and again what occurs again and once again in the Prophets: "Which I commanded not, nor spoke it, neither came it into My mind" (Jer. 19:5)—*I did not command* Jephthah to sacrifice his daughter, *I did not speak* to the king of Moab (saying) that he should sacrifice his son, *neither came it into My mind* to tell Abraham to slay his son . . . Our Rabbis say: Why in connection with the king of Moab is the verb *speak* employed? Because the Holy One, blessed be He, said: Did I ever hold a conversation with him,

---

[10] Pesikta Kahana 13a: And did he offer him up? Astrologers: No. Mesha: If miracles were performed for their sake, though he did not offer him up, all the more if he had offered him up! In Tanhuma, Ki Tissa, 5: And did he offer him up, really? Astrologers: No. Mesha: If miracles were performed for their sake though he offered him but did not really carry out the act, all the more if he had really offered him up! Yalkut, II Kings, #227: One of them at the age of a hundred had an only son, and would have offered him up before the Holy One, blessed be He, if *He had not prevented* him from doing this. Mesha: Miracles were performed for them though no offering had been made; all the more, had the offering taken place! This haggadah is known also in Christian literature; cf. L. Ginzberg, *Die Haggada bei den Kirchenvätern* (Amsterdam, 1899), pp. 83ff.

etc.? Why, I never spoke so much as a word to him—and of all things, that he is to sacrifice his son? [11]

The sum of it all is: it was clear and emphatic for the talmudic Sages that "though with Isaac there had been no completion of the act, He accepted it as genuine consummation; but what was done by Mesha was not acceptable before Him." [12]

Yet there is the verse staring us in the face, and its words toll like a bell: "And there came great wrath upon Israel" (II Kings 3:27). Both Scripture and historical fact testify and throw it into their faces, that despite statutes that are not good and ordinances not to be lived by, behold, the records and annals prove that there are idol-worshipers who go on prospering, grow old, yea, wax mighty in power. And the talmudic Sages were forced to acknowledge the facts, and to explain them some other way: By virtue of his having added a great city to Israel, three kings of his dynasty succeeded Omri on the throne. Now, there was no richer man in the world than Ahab king of Israel; two hundred and thirty-two kings were subject to him, and one of them was Mesha king of Moab. But once Ahab died, the king of Moab rebelled against the king of Israel. Against Moab's king, three kings came up; "but the moment he saw them, he took his first-born son and offered him up as a burnt offering on the altar. The Moabite king said before Him: Master of the universe, Abraham offered up his son on top of the altar *but did not slay him.* I shall slay my son and offer him up before Thee as a whole burnt offering to be completely consumed—whatever You tell me to do, I will do, as it is said (II Kings 3:27), 'Then he

---

[11] Tanhuma, ed. Buber, Wa-Yera, 40, p. 109; Aggadat Bereshit, ch. 31, p. 63. Note the different order in B. Taanit 4a: "Command" in connection with Mesha, "speak" in connection with Jephthah.

Cf. Tanhuma, ed. Buber, Be-Hukotai, 7 (end), p. 114.

[12] Gen. R. 55:5, as in the regularly printed editions.

took his first-born son' and so on. That was the moment *Israel had a fall*, from the highest station down to the lowliest station, as it is said, 'And there came great wrath upon Israel,' etc." [13]

Balaam and Mesha—not always are they shadows of a remote pagan past; on occasion they are also a symbol and example of currents of thought and polemics against beliefs and opinions in the familiar present. [14] More than all other religions of antiquity, Christianity rose to dispute the claims of Judaism and deride it, out of the new faith in the atoning power of him whom the Romans had crucified. It was especially the Cilician disciple, by trade a tentmaker in the city of Tarsus, [15] who assailed the Law and the Commandments with singular vehemence. It is he who wove together an entire system of

---

[13] Seder Eliyahu Rabba, ch. 10, ed. Friedmann, p. 50. Note how Pesikta Kahana 13b and Tanhuma, Ki Tissa, 5, and B. Sanhedrin 39b, struggle with the meaning of II Kings 3:27: "Rab and Samuel: One said, (Mesha did it) for Heaven's sake; the other said, For idolatry's sake. . . . But *re* him who says it was for idolatry's sake, why 'did a great wrath come (upon Israel)'?" An interesting interpretation from Geonic times has been preserved in a Responsum which R. Hai Gaon sent to Ḳābes (in North Africa) (cf. S. Asaf, *Mi-Sifrut ha-Geonim*, p. 153; I owe this reference to Professor Saul Lieberman): And some say that the son of the king of Edom who was to have succeeded his father on the throne was held hostage by the king of Moab: for such is protocol, that members of a royal family are held hostage by kings of similar echelon—and it was *him* that the king of Moab burned in broad daylight into *lime* (Amos 2:1), in order to throw the king of Edom into grief and

to throw Israel into grief too. This is why the verse says, "And there came great wrath upon Israel." This did *not* come from God; it was rather a *very grievous matter in the sight of Israel*. Cf. Abraham ibn Ezra and D. Kimhi *ad* II Kings 3:27 (and the wrath came upon Israel from the king of Edom): and now too see N. H. Torczyner, *Ha-Lashon we-ha-Sefer*, I, pp. 66ff., who interprets Amos 2:1 in the light of II Kings 3:27, except that he reads *mlk 'dm* as in the Canaanite inscriptions, to wit, human sacrifice. Cf. above, ch. VIII, n. 11.

[14] Cf. B. Sanhedrin 106b: A certain heretic said to Rabbi Hanina: Have you heard how old Balaam was? Said R. Hanina to him: Is it then recorded? It is not recorded, etc. He was *thirty-three* years old, etc. On the other hand, cf. Ginzberg, *JBL*, XLI (1922), 121, and idem, *Legends*, VI, 124 and 144.

[15] Acts 18:3: ἦσαν γὰρ σκηνοποιοὶ τῇ τέχνῃ.

forgiveness of sins without works of the Law, from a hybrid mixture of Jewish messianic hopes and pagan notions of gods dying and returning to life in recurring cycles.

As counterpoint to the *Akedah Story*, Paul placed the *Golgotha Event* at the heart of the new faith. If in the former there was something active for the merit of Israel, in the latter there was something active for the merit of the whole wide world, to redeem it from sin and deliver it from death, the two calamities that came down into the world through the Serpent's plotting.[16] And from these calamities there could have been neither escape nor liberation, had it not been for the compassion of the Father, who, like Abraham, did not spare His son, His favored one whom He loved, and whose life He set as ransom for the sins of all creatures. What is more, unlike Abraham He did finish what He began, and the son was crucified and died, actually died, so that those who believe in him might by his blood be forgiven and saved from the wrath.[17] The sin of one—Adam's rebellion—loaded all with guilt; the free grace of the other—the first of all created beings—came to justify all.[18] The first set in motion the cycle which leads the world to death, the second set in motion the gift of resurrection to eternal life.[19] Even as the Father raised him up to the top of the altar so that he might bear the shame of the many, so He raised him up from his sepulcher in order that to the many glory might be brought.[20] He was raised from the dead so that he would be the first of all who sleep in the dust to wake to life. And from the beginning of time this was part of the design, that the first born of Creation should be the first born of Resurrection.[21] All who are baptized in his name cleave to him, to his death

[16] Romans 5:12.

[17] Romans 8:32; cf. 3:25, 4:18-25, 5:8; Galatians 1:4; I Corinthians 15:4. Like Isaac, children of God's promise: Romans 9:7, Galatians 3:8, 4:28.

[18] Romans 5:18-19.

[19] I Corinthians 15:45-49.

[20] Galatians 3:13-14; Romans 3:23-26.

[21] Colossians 1:15-18; I Corinthians 15:20-21.

as to his rising again. With him they are crucified, so that the Evil Impulse be slain within them and the old Adam die; henceforth they are washed clean of sin and freed from the obligations of the Law's commandments.[22] With him they will rise to a new life and never again return to the pit.[23] Thus, "every one that believeth is justified from all things, from which ye could not be justified by the Law of Moses." [24]

There is here a compound heavily freighted with pagan elements, foremost of which is the ancient passion to "be like God" [25]—that dream and deep craving of the pagan world to have human beings delivered from the sentence of death and enjoying the radiance of eternity. But intertwining and amalgamating with the pagan inheritance are also hopes and expectations from the religion of Israel. In particular, there are here in fusion and confusion the story of the *Akedah*[26] and the vision of *the Servant of the Lord*,[27] smitten of God

---

[22] Romans 6:2-11, 7:1-7; Galatians 3:10-13.

[23] I Thessalonians 5:10; Acts 13:34.

[24] Acts 13:39; Romans 3:28.

[25] Gen. 3:5. And note how R. Abbahu interpreted Num. 23:19: "God is not a man, that He should lie"—If a human being says to you, I am God, he is a liar. "Neither the son of man, that He should repent" (Num. ibid.)—(If he says,) I am the son of man, he will regret it in the end. (If he says that) "I am ascending to heaven," "that is the one who speaks, but will not [carry out, promise and not] fulfill" (ibid.). J. Taanit 2:1 (end), 65b.

[26] Romans 8:32: τοῦ ἰδίου υἱοῦ οὐκ ἐφείσατο, and this is the Septuagint version of Gen. 22:12 and 16, as the Church Fathers recognized and emphasized; see Origen, *In Genes. Homil.* 8.8 (Migne, *P.G.*, XII, col. 208) and cf. Aggadat Bereshit, ch. 31,

ed. Buber, p. 64: R. Abin said in R. Hilkiah's name: How foolish is the heart of the deceivers who say the Holy One, blessed be He, has a son. If in the case of Abraham's son, when He saw that he was ready to slay him, He could not bear to look on as he was in anguish, but on the contrary at once commanded, "Don't lay your hand on the lad"; had He had a son, would He have abandoned him? Would He not have turned the world upside down and reduced it to tohubohu? This is why Solomon says (Eccl. 4:8), "There is One that is alone, and He hath not a second; yea, He hath neither son nor brother." It's only out of His love for Israel that He called them sons, as it is said (Exod. 4:2), "Israel is my firstborn son." Note also in R. Abin's name: The Nations of the World say, *We are Israel* and for our sake was the world created, etc.: Cant. R. 7:3—Gen. R. 83:5. Apparently this was the son of R. Abin

and afflicted, crushed by sins not his own and by whose stripes others are healed. From these two channels the Christian idea of atonement drew its nourishment. Its founders and teachers drew quite consciously on the reservoir of Jewish thought and expression. And what the early teachers touch on lightly comes into full view in express statements of the later ones.

Already in the Epistle of Barnabas,[28] Isaac is referred to as the prototype for the sufferings and trials of Jesus. Irenaeus exhorts Christians that in their faith they too must be on the alert to *bear the cross* just as Isaac bore the wood for the burnt-offering woodpile.[29] The Church Fathers were especially fond of this image of one bearing his own cross[30]—which occurs in midrashic-talmudic sources, as does the phrase, "Like one going out to be burned and carrying on his own shoulders the wood for his pyre." [31] It may well be that in such figures of speech is indeed reflected something of historical realities, for this was common practice, to have the condemned themselves laden with the beams and firewood by which their sen-

---

the elder (Gen. R. 58:2—The day R. Abin died, his son R. Abin was born). And in R. Hilkiah's name, R. Pinhas ha-kohen bar Hama spoke (Gen. R. 53:9); he was a contemporary of the young R. Abin, in the last generation, or one before last, of the Palestinian Amoraim. Cf. S. Buber, Aggadat Bereshit, p. 64, n. 15.

[27] II Corinthians 5:21.

[28] VII.3 (ὁ τύπος ὁ γενόμενος ἐπὶ Ἰσαάκ) cf. VII. 10 (ed. Kirsopp Lake, *The Apostolic Fathers*, I (1925); pp. 340f.).

[29] Irenaeus, *Contra haereses* IV.5.4 (Migne, *P.G.*, VII, col. 985f.): καὶ ἡμεῖς... ἄραντες τὸν σταυρὸν ὡς καὶ Ἰσαὰκ τὰ ξύλα.

[30] Tertullian, *Adversus Marcionem* III.18 (Migne, *P.L.* II, col. 346): "Isaac, cum

a patre in hostiam deditus, lignum sibi ipse portaret, Christi exitum jam tunc denotabat"; cf. *Adversus Judaeos* 10 (ibid., col. 626); Augustine, *De civ. Dei* XVI. ch. 32: "Isaac, sicut Dominus crucem suum, ita sibi ligna ad victimae locum, quibus fuerat imponendus, ipse portavit"; cf. idem, *Enarrationes in Psalmos*, Ps. 30:9 (*P.L.* XXXVI, col. 244 sq.): "Isaac, portans ligna sibi, quomodo Christus crucem portavit"; Isidorus Hisp., *Questiones in Vet. Test. in Genes. (P.L.* LXXXIII, col. 250); Beda, *Questiones super Genesim (P.L.* XCIII, col. 319); Rabanus Maurus, *Commentaria in Genesim (P.L.* CVII, col. 568).

[31] Tanhuma, ed. Buber, Wa-Yera, 46, p. 114.

tence would be carried out.[81a] Christian writers make Isaac the symbol of their faith, and so interpret the Akedah chapter as to have it serve as a foreshadowing of the death of Jesus.

So too with all the epithets originally associated with Isaac: the Christians appropriated them for their own purposes. Following Scripture, Isaac was called "the *sheep* for the burnt offering," and in his praise midrashic exegesis liked to say "that he threw himself down before his father like a sheep that is sacrificed." [32] *Lamb* sacrifices came to be interpreted as signs and reminders for Heaven, "the merits of *that sheep bound* on the altar who bared his throat for the sake of Thy Name." [33] And so too he who died on the cross came to be called the *sheep* or *lamb* slain to win by his blood redemption for all, of every nation and tongue.[34] Even more: Jesus was called "the paschal sacrifice" of the believers "who are justified by his blood." [35] Paul would spare nothing until he had converted everything he had learned from rabbinic instruction into a proclamation of the blood of the crucified Jesus acting as saving and safeguard for all who put their trust in him: for their sake he had surrendered his life to destruction, to prevent the destroyer from striking the children of his covenant. The Gospels even set the date of the death of Jesus at the Passover holiday; and we have already seen that this is also the season for the Akedah in sources which unquestionably antedate the beginnings of Christianity.[36]

Despite all the echoes of theme and vocabulary from the Holy Scriptures with which the earliest Christian Fathers tried to surround their faith, in it there was a continuation and a return of ancient pagan beliefs. The idea of the *atonement* and forgiveness

[81a] Cf. S. Lieberman, in *JQR*, XXXV (1944), 36f.

[32] Lev. R. 2:10.

[33] Targum Jonathan and Targum Jerushalmi *ad* Lev. 22:27, and cf. also *ad* Lev. 9:3: So that He might recall for your sake the merit of Isaac whom his father bound like a *lamb*.

[34] John 1:29; Revelation of John 5:6-9.

[35] I Corinthians 5:7, and cf. Romans 5:9.

[36] Cf. above, ch. VII, n. 15.

of an entire community by means of *the blood of the first born sacrificed in the first Spring month* harks back to that dim pagan antiquity which made it a practice to sacrifice the first born on the first new moon of the year—to appease and propitiate the gods, to ward off wrath and anger and fury and destruction and waste, the host of sinister angels who stand on the threshold of the new year to ravage and overthrow: they can be appealed to, they can be made to retreat, by means of a minimal gift of the sacrifice of human first born. Thus the many are saved and the whole community is forgiven and escapes through the blood of one.

We have found relics of this pagan inheritance also in the haggadah of "the blood of Isaac's Akedah." The question therefore is only natural: Did this idea reach us and Christianity from a common pagan source, an inheritance from the remote past before Scripture came into being; or did it reach us from Christianity, from direct contact with it and under its influence?

In Germany, one of the Jewish scholars of the last century did in fact conclude that the whole notion of the Akedah Merit entered Judaism from Christianity.[37] To Judaism human sacrifice is an abomination, the God Judaism talks of is in no need of substitute sacrifices or ransoms in order to be merciful toward His creatures. In Jewish belief there is no such thing as legacy of sin from one generation to the next, or transmission of sin from one man to the other; the responsibility of every creature to its Creator is unmediated. In the conception of guilt and punishment, no one can be the sin offering of another, nor provide absolution for the other. To wipe out sin there is no go-between, forgiveness does not come via agencies.

And so, this Merit of Isaac's Akedah which stands up for Israel

[37] Abraham Geiger, "Erbsünde und Versöhnungstod: deren Versuch in das Ju-   denthum einzudringen," *Zeitschrift für Wissenschaft und Leben*, X (1872), 166ff.

in every generation to effect atonement for them is "a notion in flat contradiction of the whole spirit of Judaism and is completely opposed to every one of its fundamentals." [38] Only contact and communications with the Syrian Church in Babylonia misled the Babylonian Jews to befriend this notion and then even admit it into the liturgy. There is not a trace of the idea in the Mishnah, which gave equal weight to the formula "He who answered Abraham on Mount Moriah" [39] and all similar formulae which express the gift of divine aid in the people's history or experience. So too when the Mishnah discusses the ram's-horn ceremony, it makes no mention at all of the ram in the Isaac story; all the Mishnah talks about is that the horn is to be of an antelope and straight (not curved), while the horns used in a public fast service are of rams and curved. [40] Even the view of R. Judah—who taught that on Rosh ha-Shanah, the New Year, rams' horns are used and on the (Atonement Day of the) Jubilee year antelopes' horns [41]—has been explained in the Tosefta [42] as follows: "The Sages assign the common (instrument) for the common (occasion) and the uncommon for the uncommon." The same explanation appears in the Palestinian Talmud in R. Johanan's name: "R. Judah's reasoning is, to assign the common (instrument) for the common (occasion) and the uncommon for the uncommon." [43] On the other hand, in the Babylonian Talmud this is omitted and in its place is something new: "Why is the ram's horn used? So that I might remember in your behalf the Akedah of Isaac son of Abraham." [44] This newly coined haggadic explanation (albeit in origin it is far from new and derives from alien sources) became the favorite one among the Babylonians, and it is

[38] Ibid., p. 171.
[39] M. Taanit 2:4.
[40] M. Rosh ha-Shanah 3:3-4.
[41] Ibid., 3:5.
[42] T. Rosh ha-Shanah 3:3.
[43] J. Rosh ha-Shanah 3:5 (end), 59a.
[44] B. Rosh ha-Shanah 16a.

they who incorporated it in the Rosh ha-Shanah prayers. *Tekiata*, the Alarum Sound, of Rab—this is how it is referred to. It was associated with the name of Rab, onetime head of the Sura Academy, perhaps because the institution of the rite goes back to him. This *Tekiata* exalts the attempt at human sacrifice—a weird idea and offensive to religious feeling; and it would be best to eliminate it altogether from the Prayer Book.[45]

Others came along and tried to dash this whole reasoning—it is motivated only by the passion for religious reform.[46] The order of Kingships, Memorials, Shofar-blasts (*Malkiyot, Zikronot, Shofarot*), recited as part of the Additional Prayer on Rosh ha-Shanah, was on the contrary widespread in the first Christian century; and since the Akedah motif constitutes an inseparable part of that Prayer, it is out of the question that the idea is late: it had already received expression in those days and had already been widely disseminated.[47]

Truth to say, however, it is not at all easy to fix the time of the *language* of the relevant blessings as they have come down to us:

[45] Geiger, op. cit., p. 171: "So verdanken wir Babylon und der dortigen Berührung der Juden mit den Christen die Aufnahme der Lehre von der Verdienstlichkeit des stellvertretenden und sühnenden Sohnesopfers und deren Ausprägung im Gebete für das Neujahr. . . . Befreien wir uns nun endlich von dieser babylonischen Verirrung und Verwirrung, kehren wir zu der gereinigten Lehre einer älteren Zeit zurück und läutern wir unsern Gottesdienst, indem wir Gebetstücke, welche an den Versuch eines Menschenopfers erinnern und diesen erheben, als einen unserm religiösen Bewusstsein fremdartigen und widerstrebenden Bestandteil gründlich beseitigen."

[46] Israel Lévi, "Le Sacrifice d'Isaac et la mort de Jésus," *REJ*, LXIV (1912), 161ff., 171. Hans Joachim Schoeps, "The Sacrifice of Isaac in Paul's Theology," *JBL*, LXV (1946), 385ff., 389, and M. Robinson, "Isaac's Akedah in Hebrew Literature" [in Hebrew], *Ha-Shiloah*, XXV (1911), 206ff., 312ff.

[47] Lévi, op. cit., p. 178: "le Rituel des prières de Rosch Haschana existait *déjà au Ier siècle de l'ère chrétienne*, et comme le morceau relatif à la Akèda en est une partie intégrante, on peut assurer que la doctrine qui l'inspire était déjà populaire à cette époque."

"And may there appear before Thee the Akedah to which Father Abraham subjected his son Isaac on the altar, suppressing his own feelings of pity in order to do Thy will with a perfect heart. So let Thy feelings of pity suppress Thine anger (and remove it) from us. . . . And do Thou today in compassion recall Isaac's Akedah in behalf of his offspring," etc.

In this version there is something of the language of the benediction recited by R. Ishmael ben Elisha (of the first third of the second century); hence the Sefardi Jews add the clause: "May Thy compassion suppress Thine anger, oh, may Thy compassion prevail over Thine (other) Attributes." [48] In this version there is also recollection of elements in our sources handed down at the earliest in the second generation of Palestinian Amoraim, in the second half of the third Christian century (A, B, C, D, pages 90-91).

Here then are several attempts at recording a tradition: either variant readings due to errors in the course of transcription and oral transmission; or different versions of a tradition; or additions or expansions by different homilists as they attempt to harmonize and unite kindred themes. Now, then, take note: In the name of Resh Lakish, Judah bar Nahmani held forth: "God is gone up amidst shouting, the Lord amidst the sound of the *shofar*" (Ps. 47:6)—When the Holy One, blessed be He, goes up to take His seat on the Justice Throne, He ascends in Justice, as it is written, "God (Elohim) is gone up amidst shouting"; but when Israel take hold of the *shofar* and sound it, the Holy One, blessed be He, *rises from the Justice Throne and takes His seat on the Mercy Throne*, as it is written, "The Lord (YHWH) amidst the sound of the *shofar*." He is filled with compassion for them and takes pity upon

---

[48] B. Berakot 7a. Cf. *Seder Abodat Yisrael*, ed. S. Baer (Roedelheim, 1868), p. 402.

A [49]

"*And Abraham named that site Adonai-yireh.*"

R. Bibi Rabbah in the name of R. Johanan: He said before Him, Master of the whole universe, The moment You said to me, "Take now your son, your favored one," I could have retorted, Yesterday You said to me, "For it is through Isaac that off-spring shall be continued for you," and now You say to me, "Take now." But, heaven forbid, I did not act that way; on the contrary, I suppressed my feelings of pity in order to do Thy will. So may it be Thy will, O Lord our God, whenever Isaac's children get into distress, to recall that Akedah in their behalf, and do Thou be filled with compassion for them.

B [50]

R. Bibi Rubbah in the name of R. Johanan: Father Abraham said before the Holy One, blessed be He: Master of the universe, it is manifest and known before Thee that the moment You said to me to offer up my son Isaac on the altar, I had a retort ready, to wit, Yesterday You said to me, "For it is through Isaac that off-spring shall be continued for you," and now You say to me, "And offer him there as a burnt offering." But, heaven forbid, I did not act that way; on the contrary, I suppressed my Impulse and did Thy will. So may it be Thy will, O Lord our God, whenever Isaac's children enter into distress, and there's no one to speak up as their advocate, do Thou speak up as their advocate, "Adonai-yireh," do You in their behalf be mindful of the Akedah of their Father Isaac and filled with compassion for them.

---

[49] Gen. R. 56:10 (Theodor-Albeck, p. 607). See also Yalkut, #101; Lekah Tob, p. 101; Sekel Tob, p. 69. And cf. Aggadat Bereshit, ch. 38, pp. 77 f., in R. Nehe-miah's name; but the passage is wanting in the MS; Cf. Buber's notes, ibid.

[50] J. Taanit, 2:4, 65d, L. Ginzberg, Yerushalmi Fragments, p. 176.

C [51]

R. Bibi bar Abba said in the name of R. Johanan: Father Abraham stood in prayer and supplication before the Holy One, blessed be He, and said before Him: Master of the universe, it is manifest and known before Thee: the moment You said to me, "Take now your son, your favored one," I had in my heart a retort to you, and I had in my heart something to say: Yesterday You said to me, "For it is through Isaac that offspring shall be continued for you," and now You say to me, "And offer him there as a burnt offering." On the contrary! Even as I had a retort to You and I suppressed my Impulse and made no retort to Thee, "As a deaf man hearing not,[54] as a dumb man that openeth not his mouth," so when Isaac's children get into transgression and evil deeds, do Thou make mention in their behalf of the Akedah of their Father Isaac—and rise from the Justice Throne over to the Mercy Throne—and filled with compassion for them do Thou have compassion for them —and for their sake do Thou convert the Justice Attribute into the Mercy Attribute.— When, then? "In the seventh month."

D [52]

"And Abraham named that site Adonai-yireh."

Said R.J.:[53] He said to Him: Master of the universe, it was manifest before Thee that I had a retort to You when You said to me to sacrifice Isaac. Had I retorted to You, You would have had no counterretort to me! For I could have said to You, Yesterday You said to me, "For it is through Isaac that offspring shall be continued for you," and now You say to me, Slaughter. But I made no retort to You, on the contrary, I acted like the dumb and deaf, "But as a deaf man hearing not,[54] as a dumb man that openeth not his mouth." [So] when on this day Isaac's children are on Trial before Thee—and even if any number of accusers bring charges against them—just as I held my peace and made no retort to Thee, so [too] Thou, don't listen[55] to them.

[51] Lev. R. 29:9, and the Rabbot, ed. Constantinople, 1512, and ed. Venice, 1545. Cf. also Pesikta Kahana, ch. 23, 154a-b; Yalkut, #645; MhG, Gen. 22:16, p. 359; Menorat ha-Maor, III, p. 77. And cf. Tanhuma, Wa-Yera, 23 (end); Tanhuma, ed. Buber, 46, p. 115; Yelamdenu in Yalkut Talmud Torah, Mann, p. 309.

[52] Pesikta R., first ed. (Prague, 1656), the copy in the Library of the Jewish Theological Seminary of America, which has been corrected in accordance with MS (Parma?) reading—(and what I have added on the basis of this MS I have put in brackets). Cf. Midrash Tehilim, 29:1,

ed. Buber, p. 231, and Bereshit Rabbati, p. 91.

[53] In the regularly printed editions. R. Jeremiah—a mistaken solution of the abbreviation R.J.

[54] In the first edition, yishma (third, rather than first, person); cf. Ps. 38:14.

[55] Don't (you) listen (tišma')": So the correction between the lines in that MS. But the first edition has tšwm (or tśwm). Cf. Friedmann, Pesikta R., ch. 40, 171b: (tšwh) [tśym]; perhaps this a printer's error for tswm and he corrected it to tśym. See below, nn. 66 and 67.

them, *and for their sake converts the Justice Attribute into the Mercy Attribute.* When, then? "In the seventh month, on the first day of the month." [56] This is like R. Levi's way of putting it: "All the days of the year Israel are engaged in their occupations; but on Rosh ha-Shanah they take hold of their *shofarot* and sound them before the Holy One, blessed be He, and *He rises from the Justice Throne over to the Mercy Throne,* and is filled with compassion for them. When, then? 'In the seventh month.'" [57] And this statement was inserted into the words of R. Johanan in *Leviticus Rabba.* [58]

You will find the same thing in the name of R. Hinnana bar Isaac: [59] "When you appear for Trial before Me on Rosh ha-Shanah, come with the *shofar. Then even if there are many accusers against you,* I shall recall Isaac's Akedah and acquit you." And this is repeated anonymously: "Now, what is it like with a *shofar?* A person blows into one end and the sound comes out at the other end. So too with your children. *And even if there are many accusers against them,* I let (the accusations) come in one ear and go out the other." [60] This is perhaps based on the interpretation of "at the new moon (*ḥdš*), the horn (*šwp̄r*)" (Ps. 81:4) by R. Abba or R. Berekiah ha-kohen: "Improve (*šp̄rw*) your works, give to your works a newness (*ḥdšw*), and I will become like this *shofar* for you. Even as it is with a *shofar,* a person blows into one end and the sound comes out at the other end, so as it were with all the accusations of your *accusers* before Me, I let them come in one ear and go out the

---

[56] Pesikta Kahana 151b; Lev. R. 29:3; Yalkut, ##645 and 782; Midrash Tehilim 47 (end), ed. Buber, p. 247.

[57] Lev. R. 29:10. Similarly in R. Berekiah's name, ibid., 29:6 (end): And so I rise from the Justice Throne and sit down on the Mercy Throne.

[58] Indeed, the words "and rise from the Justice Throne over to the Mercy Throne" are wanting in four sources: Pesikta Kahana, Yalkut, MhG, and Menorat ha-Maor. See above, n. 51.

[59] So read; and in Pesikta R. 167a: R. Huna bar Isaac.

[60] Pesikta R. 171b.

other." [61] The variant readings have been interchanged by the compilers of the Midrashim, and R. Johanan's words have been expanded awkwardly by citations of statements that are not his.

However, it may be surmised that all these variations originally had one feature in common: a parallelism between Abraham's conduct at the Akedah and the conduct expected in return from God, when He is appealed to, to reward His children's children. At the altar Abraham swore that he would not quit that spot until he had had his say.[62] " 'Adonai-yireh, Lord, take note' (Gen. 22:14). *Yireh*, take note—of what? He said to Him: *Lord, take note* of what I can retort!" [63] Remember everything I could have hurled upward: Is it with You, save the mark, as with men talking, who say one thing one day and another the next? [64] Yesterday You said, "But My covenant I will maintain with Isaac" (Gen. 17:21), and now You tell me to slaughter him! Where's the covenant? [65] (But,) heaven forbid, I did not act that way; on the contrary, *I suppressed my Impulse*, and made no retort to You. When Isaac's children therefore are on Trial before Thee, *"even as I held my peace and made no retort to Thee, so Thou, too, make Thou no retort to them."* [66] That is to say,

[61] Midrash Tehilim 81:5, p. 367 (R. Berekiah bar Abba, and some say, R. Berekiah in R. Abba's name); Abudraham, Rosh ha-Shanah (Warsaw, 1877), p. 145 (R. Berekiah in the name of Abba . . . All the accusers are presenting accusations before Me, etc.); Yalkut, Psalms, #831 (R. Berekiah in R. Jeremiah's name . . . So too, all who are acting the accusers against you). Cf. Lev. R. 29:6 (R. Berekiah held forth)— Pesikta Kahana 152b and 154a; Pesikta R. 166a (R. Berekiah ha-kohen), and note Friedmann *ad loc.*, n. 11.

[62] Tanhuma, Wa-Yera, 23 (end); Tanhuma, ed. Buber, ibid., 46, p. 115; Yalkut,

#101; Yelamdenu in Yalkut Talmud Torah, Mann, p. 309.

[63] Midrash Tehilim 29:1, p. 231. Cf. ibid., Psalm 119, p. 489: Yesterday You said to me, "For it is through Isaac that offspring shall be continued for you" (Gen. 21:12). Well, then, I shall sacrifice him. How now will You bless me?

[64] Yalkut, #101.

[65] See above, n. 63.

[66] So indeed R. Ephraim Zalman Margulies read in his commentary *Zera le-Ephraim* (Lwow, 1833). And so too R. David Luria in his commentary on

even as I suppressed my Impulse from retorting to You, so You too, repress Your Impulse from retorting to them! Even as I held my peace and put up (with the unbearable), so You too, hold Your peace and bear with them! Even as I made myself "like a deaf man hearing not and as a dumb man that openeth not his mouth" (Ps. 38:14), so You too, hear not "as a man that heareth not, and in whose mouth are no arguments!" [67] And out of respect these words were hushed up and their sting was removed, even though the Rabbis did not hesitate to use such a tone of voice in their comments on His patience with the wicked: Who is like Thee, O Lord, among the mute, hearing and keeping quiet! [68] And something like this is in that parable of the *shofar*: May all the accusations of all the accusers come in one ear of His and go out the other—or as the Palestinian Talmud puts it, in R. Johanan's name: "And when there is no one to speak up as their advocate, do Thou speak up as their advocate." [69]

Another version of this correspondence between high and low,

Pesikta R. (Warsaw, 1873). M. Friedmann corrected to *taśim*, that is to say, Do not pay any mind to the words of the *accusers* (in accordance with Judg. 19:30 perhaps?). Cf. Bereshit Rabbati, ed. Albeck, p. 91: When Isaac's children are on Trial on this day, even if there be any number of *accusers* presenting accusations against them, even as I kept still and made no retort to Thee, so do Thou accept nothing from these accusers; this is the intent of the verse *Adonai-yireh*, *Lord take note* of how I kept still and made no retort—*so may He be still and make no response* to the accusers.

[67] This is the continuation of the verse in Ps. 38 (vv. 14-15), see above, n. 54. "I repressed my impulse from making any retort to Thee." So the reading of MS M; cf. MhG, Genesis, ed. M. Margulies, variant readings, p. 359. See also above, n. 55. MS reading, *tiśma'*.

[68] Mekilta, ed. Friedmann, 42b (*ad* Exod. 15:11) and B. Gittin 56b (Ps. 89:9). Cf. also Aggadat Bereshit, ch. 31, p. 63: 'Bearing his silences' (literally, sheaves; Ps. 126:6), he regarded himself as a deaf-mute and held his peace. And on the lips of the *payyetanim*, regarding the Almighty: "O Mighty One, O Lord, who is like unto Thee bearing His silences"; so R. Joel of Bonn in the Threnody on the slain of Cologne, "Oh weep bitter tears": cf. B. Z. Dinaburg, *Israel in Exile* [in Hebrew], II, Book I, p. 41 (and perhaps it is to be attributed to R. Kalonymos bar Judah, first line: "The voice," Habermann, p. 65).

[69] See above, n. 50.

if one may put it that way, is preserved in Abraham's prayer, according to the *Genesis Rabba* version:[70] Even as *"I suppressed my compassion (in order) to do Thy will"*, "So may it be Thy will, O Lord my God, that *Thy compassion suppress Thine anger* against Isaac's children" [71]—(*in order*) *to do their will?*[72] Theirs? Again hand is put on mouth out of reverence for the Highest of highest.

From all these ways—in vocabulary, in imagery—of comparing Abraham's conduct with the conduct of the Shekinah, there are three things to be learned. One: Abraham's manner of speaking before God, which the homilists were so fond of, was still in a fluid state among the Palestinian Amoraim. Some recall that style in one form; some apply it another way; where one is brief another is drawn out.[73] If in fact by the second Tannaite generation there was a fixed idiom on this theme in the Memorials prayer, it is surprising that its influence is not visible in the style of the times. How can it be that the vocabulary should have failed to become an accepted form of expression in the course of one hundred and fifty years? What is further surprising: R. Johanan, and R. Bibi Rabbah who hands on the view in his name, interpret and comment on Adonai-Yireh[74] in the very language of the Rosh ha-Shanah Memorials prayer, with not a word, not a hint, that this is part of a prayer formula. One might of course reply that the ancients had not yet

[70] See above, n. 49.

[71] Cf. Lekah Tob, p. 101; in Sekel Tob, p. 70: "against my children, and the generations succeeding them."

[72] Cf. Midrash Composed under the Holy Spirit, p. 68: "Abraham stood at prayer before the Holy One, blessed be He. He said to Him: Master of the universe, when my children sin and come to grief and sound the shofar before Thee, remember Isaac's Akedah, and do what they want."

[73] Midrash Tehilim, 29, p. 231: When my children fall into transgression, remember this hour in their behalf. Cf. also Targum Jonathan and Targum Jerushalmi ad Gen. 22:14, and Targum Sheni ad Esth. 5:1.

[74] This idiom of *Adonai-yireh, Lord, take note,* etc. (Gen. 22:14) occurs also in the *Zikronot*, the Memorials prayer of the Rosh ha-Shanah Additional Prayer: "And *let there appear* before Thee the Akedah, etc."

adopted fixed formulae for the Prayer, preferring spontaneous supplication,[75] and that even as late as the last generation of the Amoraim it was customary to add something original of one's own in the Prayer.[76] If the order of Kingships, Memorials, and Shofar blasts was indeed instituted in the time of the early Tannaim,[77] then the specific formulation could not have been fully crystallized except in the course of many generations. It may well be that the formulation of the Akedah theme in the idiom of our Memorials prayer was arrived at under the influence of Abraham's prayer in R. Johanan's homily.[78]

[75] M. Berakot 4:4 and Abot 2:13.

[76] See J. Berakot 4:3, 8b: R. Aha in R. Yose's name: Something new must be added to it every day. Cf. also B. Berakot, 29b: Rabba and Rab Joseph say, both of them, He who does not know how to add something new to it.

[77] R. Johanan ben Nuri and R. Akiba disagree on the order of the Benedictions with the shofar accompaniment (M. Rosh ha-Shanah 4:5), and in Judah the practice was in accordance with R. Akiba's view, while in Galilee it was in accordance with R. Johanan's; but as late as the third generation of the Tannaim, in Usha there was no uniform practice (cf. J. Rosh ha-Shanah 4:6, 59c, and B. Rosh ha-Shanah 32a and Sifra, Emor, 11, 101d). And note Louis Finkelstein, in REJ, XCIII (1932), 12. Louis Ginzberg, REJ, XCVIII (1934), 78, suggested that the Malkiyot, Kingships, were made mandatory at Jabneh, contra R. Eliezer, who still did not regard them as an integral part of the Rosh ha-Shanah prayer; cf. B. Rosh ha-Shanah 32a and Sifre, Num., 77.

[78] This is said with reference to those who are inclined to assign an early date,

the Tannaite period, to the Malkiyot, Zikronot, and Shofarot, as does Israel Lévi, who believed that only the section "This is the day of the beginning of Thy works (of Creation)," etc. goes back to Rab, while the other parts of the M. Z. Sh. were already well established by the first Christian century (cf. p. 175, in his study noted above, n. 46). However, according to others who assign a date as late as Rab's time to the whole complex of M. Z. Sh. (cf. P. Rosenthal, Supplement 39, in Graetz's History⁴, IV, p. 471; W. Jawitz, Mekor ha-Berakot, p. 33; Elbogen, Der jüdische Gottesdienst, p. 143, and so too Hayyim Brody in his article, "M. Z. Sh. in the Prayer," in Ha-Aretz (Tel Aviv), Sept. 16, 1936 [Rosh ha-Shanah eve, 5697]), and believe that all of M. Z. Sh. from "Alenu" to the end of the Shofarot section is the handiwork of Rab's and it was he who composed it all and then disseminated it in Israel,—those others have no difficulty with the reason why the language of these Benedictions has left no recognizable traces in the various homilies on Adonai-yireh. The first to refer to Rab's Tekiata (with no mention of the author's name), is R. Samuel bar Isaac, of the

The second thing we learn is this: Even if it is said that the formulation of the Memorials prayer was influenced by a latter-day style, or that the prayer was originally composed in the period of the Amoraim, this is still no proof that the essentials and base of the idea were unknown previously. In the sources, things can be found reported in R. Johanan's name, and yet elsewhere these are to be found as antedating him by about two centuries.[79] One must therefore beware of concluding rashly that ideas about the Akedah Merit are newly come on the scene and were unknown to the ancients.

And there is still a third thing we learn: as regards the Akedah, there is nothing singular about Babylonia, and these ideas did not

---

circle of Rab Huna, Rab's successor in Sura; and from the way he puts it, perhaps it is possible to recognize that it is still a recent innovation: "Whom are we following when we pray *now*, 'This is the day of the beginning of Thy works (of Creation),'" etc. (B. Rosh ha-Shanah 27a). And as late as the last generation of the Palestinian Amoraim, the matter was still a subject for controversy: Was the world created in Tishri? R. Yose be-R. Bun felt it necessary to decide against R. Johanan's view and in accordance with R. Eliezer, because of Rab's formulation: "For it is taught in the Tekiata of Rab's *school*: This is the day of the beginning of Thy works" (J. Abodah Zarah 1:2, 39c). Now, if it was in Rab's *bet midrash*, Rab's *school*, that the *M. Z. Sh.* Benedictions in the form we have them today were instituted, perhaps it is best to say that the Jerushalmi version (under heading B; cf. above, n. 50) of R. Johanan's homily is the primary source, while the Gen. R. version (under heading A; cf. above, n. 49) may already have been influenced by the language of our Zikronot.

[79] Cf. B. Niddah 61a: R. *Johanan* said: What is the meaning of the verse (Ps. 88:6), "Among the dead, free"? When a person dies he is *free of the commandments.* Cf. Romans 7:1-6. And perhaps so too B. Berakot 34b: R. *Johanan* said: Every single one of the prophets prophesied only of the Messianic Age; but of the World to Come, "*Not an eye has seen of it,* save Thou, O God" (Isa. 64:3) (and also, B. Berakot, in that idiom: . . . to one who gives his daughter in marriage to a scholar . . . but as to the scholars themselves, *Not an eye has seen,* etc. . . . Or: to those who repent; but as to the completely righteous, *Not an eye has seen,* etc.; cf. B. Sanhedrin 99a; and see also B. Shabbat 63a, where to the reading add: R. Hiyya bar Abba said [in R. *Johanan's* name]; and so too is the reading in Yalkut, Isaiah, #508). Compare I Corinthians 2:9? But the dating of these Epistles is not without problems; cf. A. Schweitzer, *Geschichte der Paulinischen Forschung* (1911), pp. 92ff.

spread over Judaism because of contact with Syrian Christians. We
have seen plainly that in Palestine early Amoraim no less than late
ones were all ears for the thought of the Akedah Merit. It is even
possible to add to the evidence, and prove that the Palestinian
Sages believed the Merit of the Akedah perseveres in every generation; and they even tried to support this with biblical proof-texts.
One consonant in the Akedah composition was enough of a peg for
their purposes. "And Abraham lifted up his eyes, and looked, and lo,
behind, 'hr, a ram" (Gen. 22:13). What is the meaning of this 'hr?
It should be 'hd (one ram)! The fact is, the reading " 'yl 'hd," "one
ram," has survived both in the Aramaic versions and in the statements of the talmudic Sages;[80] and some even held that reading to
be the correct one. Howbeit, this tiny difference in the shape of the
d and r (ר, ד), what delightful things it can release in the Torah,
what cheer it brings! That word 'hr is a deliberate inversion, for a
lesson!—that Abraham lifted his eyes to the 'hryt, the End of days.[81]
" 'hr, (a ram) caught in the thicket by his horns": Said the Holy
One, blessed be He, to Father Abraham, 'hr, after many generations, in the future your children will be caught in sins and entangled in all kinds of distress; but in the end they will be redeemed
by the horns of the ram, as it is said (Zech. 9:14), "And the Lord
shall be seen over them . . . and the Lord God will blow the
horn," [82] etc.

This midrash was presented in several versions and in the name
of any number of Sages—for example, in the name of R. Levi,[83]

[80] See above, n. 6.

[81] So put by R. Joshua ibn Shuaib,
Derashot, Wa-Yera. Cf. Lekah Tob, p.
99: " 'hr," a signal to Israel of the end
of ('brit) the exile.

[82] J. Taanit 2:4, 65d, and Gen. R. 56:9:
"R. Judah bar Simon said." L. Ginzberg,

Yerushalmi Fragments, p. 176: "R. Judan
bar Shalom said." In Yalkut Makiri,
Zech. 9:14: "R. Judah bar Simon said
in R. Johanan's name."

[83] Gen. R., loc. cit. (and in his name a
different view in Lev. R. 29:10); and in
Jerushalmi, loc. cit., in the name of R.

one of R. Johanan's disciples. It was because our Father, Abraham, saw the ram making his getaway from one thicket, but getting entangled in another thicket, that the Holy One, blessed be He, said to him: This is the way your children will get entangled in the future, in one empire after another—out of Babylonia into Media, out of Media into Greece, out of Greece into Edom! Said he before Him: Master of the universe, is this to go on forever? Said He to him: No, for in the end they will be redeemed by the horns of the ram, as it is written (Zech. 9:14, 15), "And the Lord God will blow the horn . . . the Lord of Hosts will come to their defense."

Or in the name of R. Hinnanah bar Isaac:[84] "All year long Israel are in the grip of sin and entangled in distress; but on Rosh ha-Shanah they take hold of the *shofar* and sound the blast, and are brought to mind before the Holy One, blessed be He, and He forgives them." And so too anonymously and with extra emphasis on the Akedah Merit: The Holy One, blessed be He, said to Abraham, "Take note of what is before you, your children who will appear after you: when they are entangled in sin and caught in its grip, what are they to do with his horns? They are to take these horns and sound the blast; and I shall bring to mind Isaac's Akedah and acquit them at the Trial."[85]

Perhaps it is no accident that we find this thought expressed especially in R. Johanan's circle; like him, Resh Lakish also taught such a lesson, and his *Turgeman*, his dragoman, too, Judah bar Nahman,[86] and of R. Johanan's disciples R. Levi[87] also, and R. Abbahu: and he is the one quoted in the Babylonian Talmud, "Why

---

Hinnanah bar Isaac; in Lev. R., loc. cit., R. Huna bar Isaac, and cf. Pesikta Kahana 154b.

[84] Gen. R., loc. cit.; and cf. n. 79.

[85] Pesikta R. 171b, and cf. Tanhuma, Wa-

Yera, 23 (end) and Tanhuma, ed. Buber, Wa-Yera, 46, p. 115.

[86] See above, n. 56.

[87] See above, n. 57.

is the ram's horn used? So that I might remember in your behalf the Akedah of Isaac son of Abraham." [88] And so too R. Bibi, [89] R. Abbahu's disciple. And you will find the like also among R. Johanan's teachers, in the last Tannaite generation and the beginning of the Amoraic period. The Tanna R. Benaiah who commented on the Akedah, [90] and on the Merit of the Akedah, [91] was R. Johanan's teacher. [92] The explanation of ceremonies of the public fast service as remembrance of Isaac's ashes or the Merit of the Akedah comes from the circle or in the name of R. Hanina *major*, [93] the distinguished disciple of Rabbi (Judah the Prince) and another teacher of R. Johanan. So too R. Hoshaya Rabba, the father of Mishnah, on whom R. Johanan also attended, spoke in lavish praise of Isaac: Why is it that Abraham spent time outside the Land, Jacob spent time outside the Land; but Isaac was never given permission to leave it? The Holy One, blessed be He, said to Isaac: *You are an unblemished whole burnt offering*, which, if it goes on the other side of the Veil, becomes disqualified! [94] Which is another way of saying, on the altar Isaac was found acceptable and became *sanctissimus*, and *that* does not go outside the Temple court.

That the glory of Isaac exceeds that of the other Patriarchs we hear also from R. Jonathan, he too one of those close to the circle of R. Hanina of Sepphoris, where R. Johanan was born and was active. Two interpretations of one verse by two Sepphoris Sages have fortunately been preserved, the one from the third Tannaite generation and the other from the first Amoraic generation. And perhaps

---

[88] See above, n. 44.

[89] See above, n. 49.

[90] Gen. R. 56:9; see above, ch. VIII, nn. 5-6.

[91] Gen. R. 55 (end); see below, n. 139.

[92] B. Baba Batra 57b.

[93] B. Taanit 16a, cf. above, ch. V, n. 20.

[94] Gen. R. 64:3 and Yalkut, #111; cf. MhG, Toledot, Gen. 26:2, Tanhuma, ed. Buber, Toledot, 6, p. 128, Wa-Yishlah, 10, p. 168. See also Ibn Shuaib, Hayye Sarah, 9c.

we may be able to deduce something regarding the change in the climate of opinion that took place among the scholars in the course of one hundred years, more or less.

Israel said (Isa. 63:16), "For Thou art our Father; for *Abraham* knoweth us not, and *Israel* doth not acknowledge us; Thou, O Lord, art our Father, our Redeemer from everlasting is Thy Name." And Isaac, why is he missing? R. Yose bar Halafta interpreted this to Isaac's discredit, because he blessed Esau and said to him (Gen. 27:40), "But when you grow restive, you shall throw off his yoke from your neck": (that is,) If you see your brother Jacob throwing off the yoke of the Torah from his neck, decree *shemad*, devastation, against him and you will dominate him. That is why Isaac is not mentioned along with the other Patriarchs: "he who tells Esau to decree *shemad* against (Jacob)—you mention him in the same breath with Patriarchs?" [95]

On the other hand, in R. Samuel bar Nahmani's statement in the name of his teacher R. Jonathan, that Isaiah verse is interpreted to Isaac's credit: In the Age to Come the Holy One, blessed be He, will say to Abraham, Your sons have sinned. Says Abraham before Him, Then let them be wiped out for the sake of Thy holy Name. Thereupon God says, I'll speak to Jacob; after all, he knew the difficulties of raising children; perhaps he will beseech mercy for them. God says to him, Your sons have sinned. Says Jacob before Him, Then let them be wiped out for the sake of Thy holy Name. At which God says: The aged are without sense and the young are empty of good counsel. God says to Isaac: Your sons have sinned. Says Isaac before Him, Master of the universe, *My* sons, not *Thy* sons? On the occasion when, before they even said "We will listen," they first exclaimed "We will put into practice," You called them (Exod. 4:22) "My son, My first born." Now they are my sons!

---

[95] Gen. R. 67:7.

And not *Thy* sons? Moreover, how many years are allotted to a man? Seventy years. Subtract twenty, because Thou dost not punish (misconduct in) them—that leaves fifty. Subtract twenty-five years of nighttime—leaves twenty-five. Subtract twelve and a half taken up with prayer, eating, and attention to nature's needs—leaves twelve and a half. Are You ready to put up with all of it? Fine. Otherwise, You take half and I'll take half. And if You wish, *I'll take on the whole amount*—here is my life as an offering before Thee! At which Israel exclaim, "For thou art our father" (Isa. 63:16). Says Isaac to them: Instead of acclaiming me, acclaim the Holy One, blessed be He. And with his own gaze Isaac shows them the Holy One, blessed be He. Immediately they lift their eyes upward and say: "Thou, O Lord, art our Father, our Redeemer from everlasting is Thy Name" (ibid.).[96]

In this midrash you indeed hear Isaac's full praise: how he is ever ready and on the alert to act as the advocate of Israel, and, if need be, their atonement sacrifice. And perhaps from inside that midrash you can hear a faint sound—possibly something even softer than faint sound—of religious polemics: a hint that is not even a hint at the difference between Isaac's sons and those who deify anyone save "the Lord, our Father, our Redeemer from everlasting is Thy Name."

You will discover that generations differ: one praises principally the father who brought the offering, another the son who was to be the offering. And sometimes there was even a give-and-take over the matter: whose powers were superior? "Of the two, who was the superior in performance? Was it Abraham who with his own hands was prepared to slaughter his son, or was it Isaac who cast all thought of himself to the winds and offered himself to be slaughtered?"[97] For the most part, it was Abraham's merits they

---

[96] B. Shabbat 89b, Yalkut, Isaiah, #508.   [97] R. Bahya, Wa-Yera: "So worthy was

magnified, especially in the Middle Ages. But in an ancient source, in the Memorials prayer of Rosh ha-Shanah, it is said: "And in compassion do Thou recall today unto *his* seed Isaac's Akedah." [98] And this may be the reason why the talmudic Sages sought to emphasize that—all the more glory to Isaac—he was thirty-seven years old when he was bound on the altar,[99] and the father would never have been able to tie him down if he had been unco-operative.[100] Indeed, it was of his own free will, without any compulsion whatsoever, out of rejoicing at having a *mitsvah* to perform, that he carried out the will of his father on earth and the will of his Father in heaven. Shall his reward be anything less than total?

You might be inclined to say that all this encomium on the righteousness, yea sanctity[101] too, of the son who is to be the offering, comes as a result of Christian influence—or to *dispute* the Christian claim. Maybe; and again, maybe not. For Judaism had to contend not only with Christianity but with all the religions and civilizations of the ancient Near East. Against them too Judaism entered the lists, them too it sought to refute; and it happened that wittingly and unwittingly it borrowed from them too. Jews, Christians—neither escaped pagan influences. Pagan legends and fancies regarding gods who died and from death rose again to life shaped the redemption *mythos* of the Christians. Is it conceivable that nothing of this ancient heritage or of the pagan milieu survived and settled in Judaism as well?

This may explain at least partially *a number of parallels* in the accounts by the two faiths of the happenings at Moriah and Gol-

---

Abraham, had he had a hundred bodies, he might well have surrendered them all for Isaac's sake."

[98] Cf. Ginzberg, *Legends*, V, 249.

[99] Seder Olam, ch. 1, ed. Alexander Marx, p. 4, and notes. Cf. Midrash Lamentations, Petihata 24, ed. Buber, p. 27;

Tanhuma, Wa-Yera, 21, and Tanhuma, ed. Buber, Wa-Yera, 46, p. 114; PRE, ch. 31.

[100] Gen. R. 56:5; see the reading of the regularly printed editions.

[101] See above, n. 94.

gotha. Note well *Satan's* battle at the Akedah and at the sacrifice
of the Christian savior. Early Christian literature loves to tell that
Jesus vanquished the forces of evil by cleverly taking on the sem-
blance of flesh and blood and appearing like a human being; thus
he succeeded in getting himself crucified that thereby "through
death he might break the power of him who had death at his command, that is, the devil." [102] Among the Jews also forces of destruction are equated and united: "He is Satan, he is the Evil Impulse,
he is the angel of death." [108] Among the Jews, too, that accuser seeks
with all his might and cunning to prevent and undo the Akedah.
And the talmudic Sages, with their creative haggadic imagination,
understood well how to lay bare Satan's wiles.

Samael overtakes Father Abraham on his way to Mount Moriah.
To the patriarch he appeared in the figure of an old man and said
to him: Where are you going? Abraham said to him: To pray.
Samael: What's the wood, the fire, and the knife for? Abraham
realized that he would not be able to put him off; he therefore said
to him, "I go in mine integrity" (Ps. 26:1) to do the will of my
Father in heaven.

SAMAEL: And what did your Father say to you?

ABRAHAM: To offer up my son before Him as a burnt offering.

SAMAEL: Grandfather, Grandfather, are you out of your mind!
You are going to slaughter the son who was born to you when you
were a hundred years old?

ABRAHAM: Those are the terms!

SAMAEL: An elder of your years to make such a mistake! He
ordered this only to mislead and deceive you! Lo, it is written in
the Torah (Gen. 9:6), "Whoever sheds the blood of man, by man
shall his blood be shed"; and you are going to slaughter your son?

[102] Hebrews 2:14.
[108] Statement by Resh Lakish in B. Baba
Batra 16a.

If you say to Him, Thou Thyself didst so order me—He will say to you: What witnesses to that effect have you? Besides, even if you have witnesses, no testimony of a slave against his master is of any worth!

ABRAHAM: I'm not listening to you. I am going ahead to do the will of my Father in heaven. . . .[104]

The Sages tied together the two uses of *nsh* and interpreted the verb *nsh, put to the test,* used in connection with Abraham (Gen. 22:1), and *nsh, venture,* in Job 4:1. There are many approaches adopted in the treatment of this theme, and a whole bundle of authorities. We will refer to a few of them in the chronological sequence of Amoraic times, as preserved in a midrashic fragment discovered among the Genizah manuscripts.[105]

R. Yose ben Zimrah, a contemporary of Rabbi (Judah the Prince), said: "This is how Satan talked to Abraham—Are you not he at whose door all the grandees of the world assemble at dawn in order to benefit from your counsel? If you carry out this act, they will all forsake you ever after. Turn back! But Abraham would pay no heed to his advice."

R. Eleazar ben Pedat, a disciple of R. Haninah and R. Hoshaya, and a colleague-disciple of R. Johanan, said: "This is how Satan talked to Abraham—Are you not he at whose presence all princes rise to their feet? And when they're riding their horses, dismount before you and bow down to you? If you carry out this act, all the

[104] Gen. R. 56:4; Yalkut, #98; Midrash Composed under the Holy Spirit, Mann, p. 63; MhG, p. 306. And note Satan's attempts at seducing *Isaac*: Yalkut, loc. cit.; Tanhuma, Wa-Yera, 22 and Tanhuma, ed. Buber, Wa-Yera, 46, p. 114; Pesikta R. 170b; Midrash Wa-Yosha, p. 36. And cf. PRE, ch. 32: Satan fell into a fury when he saw that his passionate wish to thwart Abraham's sacrifice was powerless. What did he do? He went and told *Sarah,* etc. She wept 3 times corresponding to the 3 *tekiot,* etc. Cf. parallels, and above, ch. VIII, n. 43.

[105] Midrash Composed under the Holy Spirit, Mann, pp. 63ff. This is the source drawn upon by MhG, Gen., beginning of ch. 22.

bowings before you will turn into bootings—for it is said (Job 4:4),
'Thy words have upholden him that was falling, and thou hast
strengthened the feeble knees.' [Turn back! But Abraham would
pay no heed to his advice.]"

R. Johanan said: "This is how Satan talked to Abraham—If you
get to the point of striking the blow and then recoil, by all rights
He can charge you, saying, You accepted slaughtering him from
the very first moment (of my command)! What retort can you
(then) make? As it is said (Job 4:5), 'But now it is come unto thee,
and thou art weary; it toucheth thee, and thou art affrighted.' "
[Turn back! But Abraham would pay no heed to his advice.]

R. Simeon ben Lakish said: "This is how Satan talked to Abraham—The very fear of Heaven that's in you is your folly, as it is
said (Job 4:6), 'Is not thy fear of God thy folly?' So satanically
did Satan act against Abraham, but he could not prevail over him."

Now all these statements and many like these were abbreviated
in the Gemara in the most extreme fashion, and the very names of
the authors were suppressed.[106] If that single fragmentary source
(from the Genizah) had not survived, would not your impulse have
driven you—in the light of the more copious stories in Christian
literature—to decide that such statements derive from that? And
would you not have speculated, Maybe only in Amoraic times, as
a result of Christian influence, Israel's teachers said what they said?
Fortunately there is preserved also a homily from Tannaite times.
R. Simeon ben Yohai said: This is how Satan talked to Abraham
—Why, this son of yours is the spit-and-image of you! What kind
of man sticks a knife into himself?[107]—Indeed, this is an ingenious
interpretation of Job 4:5, "It toucheth thee, and thou art affrighted":

[106] B. Sanhedrin 89b and cf. Rashi, ibid.,
as well as his commentary ad Job 2:4:
he was in possession of trustworthy traditions.

[107] Mann, p. 64, and MhG, p. 347.

that is to say, Are you going to touch your son, *your own flesh*, with evil intent and not be affrighted?

But above all—this business of Satan or Prince Hatred is already mentioned in the *Book of Jubilees*,[108] which is certainly earlier than Christianity.

How cautious we must be even with strange expressions in our sources, and it is in vain we undertake to erase or emend these. In the *Midrash Tanhuma* this is how the conversation is pictured, between the father on the quick to make the sacrifice and the son on the quick to be the sacrifice: "Forthwith both of them built the altar; and (Abraham) bound (Isaac) on the altar, and took the knife to slaughter him so that a quarter of his blood should be released. Along came *the Satan* and pushed Abraham's hand, so that the knife fell out of his hand. And when (Abraham) stretched forth his hand to recover the knife, a *Bat Kol* from heaven issued and called to him: 'Do not raise your hand against the lad.' If not for that, the lad would have been butchered." [109] What's *Satan* doing here? Should it not be *the angel?* [110] But the texts are not to be tampered with, for we have here the remains of an additional detail in the stories of the wiles and wars of Satan, stories which have been cut down, abridged, and possibly altogether withdrawn from our literature—in the first place, in order to have nothing contradicting what the Torah says plainly in regard to the Akedah; in the second place, to deprive heretics of any excuse to say, It seems that on high there are two Dominions. Nevertheless, here a speck and there a speck survives, stray traces of *the Epic of the Contest of Satan at the Akedah*, a haggadic product of folk imagination, taking sip and sustenance from pagan streams and ancient Persian beliefs regarding the war of light and darkness. And what-

[108] 17:16f. and 18:9 and 12.

[109] Tanhuma, Wa-Yera, 23.

[110] Cf. Ginzberg, *Legends*, V, 251.

ever of this alien heritage could be converted to Judaism's purposes
was admitted and permitted in the various homilies to serve as
fragrance and spice for the essentials of Torah and the commandments. Sometimes you can not even recognize that the details come
from a distance, and they appear as proper as proper can be. "And
Abraham built an altar there" (Gen. 22:9). Now, why did not
Isaac build along with him? Because Abraham feared lest *there fall*
on the lad a stone or a piece of stone and blemish him, and thus
he would become disqualified for sacrifice.[111] But according to an
earlier wording—This was not (fear of) an accident; it was (out
of fear of) Satan's bag of tricks. "And Abraham built . . . there."
And where was Isaac? Said R. Levi: "Abraham had put him out of
sight; he thought: *Best that that one to be rebuked* (Zech. 3:3)
not throw a stone and disqualify the lad for sacrifice."[112]

Here can be noticed also the difference between the two faiths.
To Paul, Satan appeared as though he were "the prince of the
power of the air, the spirit now at work among the children of
disobedience,"[113] and is "the god of this age":[114] "For our battle is
not against flesh and blood, but against principalities, against powers, against potentates of this dark world, against the host of spirits
of wickedness in the heavenly places."[115] In Jewish sources, into
Satan's power no such strength or autonomy, no such dominion or
possessions either below or on high, is granted. To be sure, "he
comes down and seduces, and goes up and stirs up wrath"—but
he must also "get leave."[116] In the Book of Jubilees,[117] and so too in
haggadic traditions from R. Johanan in R. Yose ben Zimrah's

---

[111] Pesikta R. 170b.
[112] Gen. R. 56:5. See Tosafot al ha-Torah,
Hadar Zekenim (= *Bet ha-Midrash*, ed.
Jellinek, V, 157): The Midrash has it
that he put him into a chest until the
time he planned to slay him, because he
feared lest the Satan blemish him in some

way.
[113] Ephesians 2:2.
[114] II Corinthians 4:4.
[115] Ephesians 6:12.
[116] B. Baba Batra 16a.
[117] 17:16.

name,[118] Satan talks God into putting Abraham to the test, as it is said also in the Book of Job, and "were it not for the biblical verse black on white, it would be impossible to say (that God is prevailed on) as a human being is enticed by enticers." [119] However, in R. Johanan's academy, his disciples could find no rest until they got to the bottom of Satan's intention and occupation. R. Levi said: "Satan and Peninah had only Heaven's sake in mind. When Rab Aha bar Jacob repeated this in a homily in Paphunia, Satan came and kissed his feet." [120]

One more parallel in the line of narratives of the Akedah and the Crucifixion: both are tied to the idea of the *Resurrection of the Dead*. He is Satan, he is the angel of death;[121] and the victor over Satan is the victor over death: for himself he gains and through him others gain eternal life. Not for nothing did the Haggadah attach Isaac's righteousness to the "Resurrection of the Dead" Benediction (in the Shemoneh Esreh Prayer).[122] In the Christian faith, too, it was an important principle that by the sacrifice of the crucified one, Satan, or the angel of death, lost dominion over the believers, for in the blood of their savior they won atonement and by his merit they were destined for a new life, even as he rose on the third day after his burial, as recounted in the Gospels.[123] Christian literature is brimful of this subject; in our sources there are only hushed hints.

"After two days will He revive us, *on the third day* He will raise us up, that we may live in His Presence" (Hos. 6:2). By what

---

[118] B. Sandhedrin 89b: R. Johanan said in the name of R. Yose ben Zimrah. Cf. Mann, p. 65, and MhG, beginning of ch. 22; see also Gen. R. 55:4. And note the Yemenite Yalkut, Maayan Gannim, MS, cited in M. M. Kasher, *Torah Shelemah*, p. 902, #151. See also below, n. 148: *The Justice Attribute*.

[119] Statement by R. Johanan: B. Baba Batra 16a; cf. B. Hagigah 5a.

[120] B. Baba Batra 16a. See also Yalkut, I Samuel, #77 and Yalkut, Job, #893 (Let no man try to be more devout than Abraham). Cf. also MhG, Gen. 22:1, p. 348.

[121] See above, n. 103.

[122] See above, ch. IV.

[123] Matthew 17:23; Luke 24:7. Cf. I Corinthians 15:4, etc.

merit? The Masters and R. Levi: The Masters say, By merit of the Giving-of-Torah on the third day (Exod. 19:16); R. Levi said, By merit of the third day of Father Abraham (Gen. 22:4).[124] And was something similar perhaps said of the Messianic King as well, and omitted for fear of disputations with Christians?[125]

"And we will worship and we will return to you" (Gen. 22:5): his own mouth announced to him that both of them would return in peace.[126] R. Isaac said: Everything, thanks to worship. Abraham returned from Mount Moriah only by virtue of (his) worshiping, etc. The Torah was given only by virtue of worship, etc. The dead will live again only by virtue of worship.[127] And some even read the text or interpreted it so that everything is won by virtue of *that* worshiping of Father Abraham: "By virtue of *this* worship his sons were found worthy of 'You shall worship from afar' (Exod. 24:1), and *by it* they will merit the reassembling of the exiles, 'and they shall worship the Lord in the holy mountain at Jerusalem' " (Isa. 27:13).[128] If that's the case, then, will the dead come to life again by virtue of *this* worship? And is this disciple of R. Johanan too, R. Isaac Napha,[129] like R. Levi, hanging the Resurrection of the Dead on the Akedah Merit?

Perhaps it is an ancient tradition which is being explained by the

[124] Gen. R. 56 (beginning), Yalkut, #99 and Yalkut, Joshua, #12.

[125] Cf. Raymond Martini, *Pugio Fidei* (ed. Carpzov, Leipzig, 1687), p. 877, and see Saul Lieberman in *Sheki'in*, pp. 59, 61, in *re* the Messiah that in the future he will put Satan to utter shame and cast him into Gehenna (see Pesikta R. 161b) and "not a Satan will remain in the world" (Abudraham, Rosh ha-Shanah, p. 144), "and death will be pulled up by its roots out of the world, as it is said (Isa. 35:8), 'He will swallow up death forever' " (*Arugat ha-Bosem*, I, p. 262). And cf.

Midrash Wa-Yosha, p. 56: And how do we know that the Judgment will take place on the third day? For it is said (Hos. 6:2), "After two days He will revive us, on the third day He will raise us up," etc.

[126] Tanhuma, Wa-Yera, 13, and parallels.

[127] Gen. R. 56:2.

[128] Lekah Tob, p. 98.

[129] Cf. B. Zebahim 62a: R. Isaac Napha on Isaac's ashes, see above, ch. V, n. 21. In Midrash Hadash al ha-Torah (Mann, p. 163): R. Berekiah is the speaker.

midrash (regardless of what its age is): [130] "By virtue of Isaac who offered himself as a sacrifice on top of the altar, *the Holy One, blessed be He, will quicken the dead in the future,* as it is said (Ps. 102:21), 'To hear the groaning of him who is bound; [to open up release for the offspring appointed to death].' " *Him who is bound* is interpreted as Isaac bound on top of the altar; *to open up release for the offspring appointed to death,* as the dead whose graves the Holy One, blessed be He, will open up so that He may set them on their feet in the Age to Come. Another verse like this one (Ps. 79:11), "Let the groaning of him that is bound come before Thee; according to the greatness of Thy power set free the offspring appointed to death," served already in the second Tannaite generation as the basis for R. Joshua's comments on "Isaac ben Abraham, who gave a quarter of blood on the altar," and by virtue of it the Holy One, blessed be He, sought to loose the fetters of Isaac's sons in Egypt. And is it possible that it was further explained that by this virtue the Holy One, blessed be He, will in the future preserve them and restore them to life in that world which is altogether without terminus? [131]

On the subject of the third day of Resurrection, the Midrashim are rather meager, but the Gospels are rich with information. Attend well: it may be that from this poverty of explicit statement, and perhaps also from the silence growing out of caution, you will hear the voice which is the voice of Jacob crying out because of what the hands which are the hands of Esau have done to him. Much did our fathers suffer when priests and apostates forced them into disputations before kings and pontiffs, to prove from talmudic

[130] Cf. Pesikta Kahana 200b, and Israel Lévi's study referred to above, ch. VI, n. 8.

[131] Mekilta Simeon, Wa-Era, ed. Hoffmann, p. 4; see above, ch. VI, n. 6. Cf. also Yalkut Reubeni, Wa-Yera (in the name of Maggid, Toledot pericope): If Abraham had not subjected his son Isaac to Akedah, there would be no Resurrection of the dead.

literature that the messiah had already come. This is why Jews shut their doors and Christians threw theirs wide open to the theme of the third day of Resurrection.

But it is certain that the very notion goes back essentially to times long before Christianity, and before Judaism no less. This three-day season between the death and resurrection of the gods was well known to many nations in the ancient Near East. The Babylonian Tammuz and Osiris, the god of the Egyptians—among others—go down to the nether world and come up again on the third day.[182] It may be that such a belief grew out of experience, actual observation of corpses, that after three days their facial features begin to decompose. Hence the laws in the event of death and the mourning customs of the ancient world: "The height of the mourning period lasts for the first three days. Why? Because the shape of the face is still recognizable (that long); for we learn in the Mishnah: In testimony regarding the identity of a dead man, what counts is only recognition of the features of the face with the nose still part of it—(nothing else,) even if other bodily signs or his garments are identified. And after three days, there is no acceptable testimony." [183] In the skies too the ancients could observe this period, that the moon gets overcast, as though it had died, and then returns anew after three days.[184] That is why this interval was such a favorite and became widespread in fasting rituals, temple cults, miracle stories, witchcraft, and also in beliefs about that wonder world of

[182] Erich Ebeling, *Tod und Leben nach den Vorstellungen der Babylonier* (1931); see, especially, no. 11; Hugo Gressmann, *Tod und Auferstehung des Osiris* (1923); W. Baumgartner, "Der Auferstehungsglaube im alten Orient," *Zeitschrift für Missionskunde und Religionswissenschaft,* XLVIII (1933), 213 [now reprinted in his *Zum Alten Testament und seiner Umwelt* (Leiden, 1959), pp. 124-146].

[183] Lev. R. 18:1 and Gen. R. 73:5. Cf. Tanhuma, Mi-Keṣ, 4, and Midrash Ecclesiastes 12:6. See too B. Moed Katan 21b and B. Shabbat 152a, J. Moed Katan 3, 82a and J. Yebamot 16, 15c.

[184] W. von Baudissin, *Adonis und Esmun* (1911), pp. 413ff.; Baumgartner, op. cit., p. 195.

Resurrection of the Dead. "After two days will He revive us, on the third day He will raise us up, that we may live in His Presence" (Hos. 6:2) was already an old old saying in the days of the prophet, and it was taken over from ancient fasting and mourning customs, to express the hope of the people's rising again after its defeat and downfall (in the days of Rezin and ben Remaliahu).[185] And quite possibly even at that date this imagery and manner of speaking were so customary and common that no one was sensitive any longer to their pagan roots or origin.

At all events, here is clear testimony that at least as early as the eighth century before the Christian era and the birth of Christianity, pagan conceptions of gods dying and returning to life in countless cycles of death and life were widely known among the people. Out of such beliefs sprouted the hopes and traditions of ancient peoples that perhaps for mortals too it might be possible to gain the lot of an endlessly renewed life.[186] Such hankerings and conceits were at the very center of the religious life of the ancient Near East, and they achieved genuine popularity in the pagan festivals, so that they became a commonplace in the whole ancient world. And some dust from the world of idolatry settled on us as well. This leftover from the province of heathendom, which was of minor consequence in Israel, became the central concern of the Christians, who sought to restore it to its pristine power and relevance. Be all this as it may, even this parallel between Moriah and Golgotha does not establish necessarily a straight line of dependence or mutual influence; and it may even be that the underlying notions are much older, going back to a common heritage of pagan beliefs.

---

[185] See my paper on this Hosea chapter in the *Harvard Theological Review*, XXVII (1934), 131ff.

[186] Cf. *Epic of Akhat* in the texts from Ugarit, correctly explained by H. L. Ginsberg, *Bulletin of American Schools of Oriental Research*, XCVII-XCVIII (1945). See *Louis Ginzberg Jubilee Volume*, English vol., p. 314.

Note also the *differentiae* of the two visions, for possibly from these there is a lesson to be learned or an inference to be made. The Akedah was not permitted to make a breach in the wall of the faith articulated by the benediction formula "who remembers the *mercies of the Fathers* and brings *a redeemer* to their children's children." [187] Whatever might have proved toxic in the praises lavished upon the Akedah victim, an antidote will be found for it: *The Patriarchs are one and all alike,* this one and that one.[188] Many were the merits the talmudic Sages hung on the Akedah, but they did not neglect to mention also the merits of other righteous men, never did they set up all salvation and hope of Israel on one man's grace in times gone by. R. Benaiah can offer the following exposition: " *'And he split* the logs for the burnt offering' (Gen. 22:3): as a reward for Father Abraham's splitting and splitting the logs for the burnt offering, he merited having the Holy One, blessed be He, split (the waves of) the Sea before his children, as it is said (Exod. 14:21), 'The waters were split.' " [189] But so too Simeon of Kitron can set up a relationship between similar consonants in Scripture for his midrashic exposition: The Sea was rent asunder because of Joseph—"The Sea saw it *and fled (wyns)*" (Ps. 114:3) by virtue of "*And (he) fled (wyns)* and got him out" (Gen. 39:12).[140]

A kind of advocacy and pardon for Israel is lodged in the Akedah, and it causes the rising from the Justice Throne over to the Mercy Throne. "A cluster of henna *(kpr)*' (Cant. 1:14): *a cluster* refers to Isaac, who was tied together on the altar like a cluster; *henna*

---

[187] The Abot (Fathers) Benediction in the Prayer; and it does not occur in the old Palestinian version published by S. Schechter, JQR, X (1898), 656.

[188] Tosefta Keritot, end, p. 567; Mekilta, Bo, beginning; Gen. R. 1, end.

[189] Gen. R. 55 (end). Cf. also Mekilta, Be-Shallah, II, 3; Mekilta Simeon *ad* Exod., 14:15; Exod. R. 21:8.

[140] Gen. R. 87:8. Cf. Gen. R. 84:5 and Mekilta, loc. cit.

(kpr), because he atones for (kpr) the iniquities of Israel."[141] But something of this power up on high belongs as well to the *ṣaddikim*, the righteous ones, of every generation. That "the death of the righteous ones acts as atonement"[142] does not exhaust the matter; even in their lifetime "the prayers of the righteous reverse the attributes of the Holy One, blessed be He, the Wrath Attribute becomes the Compassion Attribute."[143] What is the virtue of the Akedah? *"Adonai-yireh, Lord, take note"*: when Isaac's children lapse into sin and evil deeds, He takes note and recalls Isaac's Akedah and converts the Justice Attribute into the Mercy Attribute for their sake. This indeed He promised, however: that He will take note too of the good works of every pure one and saint in the chain of all generations: " 'I am a shield to you' (Gen. 15:1), from you I shall set up any number of *shields of righteous men*. Not only that, but when your children lapse into sin and evil deeds, I look to one righteous man in their midst who will be able to say to the Justice Attribute: Enough, now! Him I take up and atone for them."[144]

Even more. There is nothing fixed even about the Akedah's effects, and there are times when its virtues fail because of Israel's iniquities. R. Hinanah bar Isaac said:[145] "So long as Abraham was engaged in the Akedah of his son down below, on high the Holy One, blessed be He, kept tying the hands of the Princes of the Nations. But that is not how they remained. On the contrary, when

[141] Cant. R. 1:14.

[142] B. Moed Katan 28a, J. Yoma 1:1, 38b.

[143] B. Yebamot 64a. Cf B. Sukkah 14a: The prayer of the righteous turns the intention of the Holy One, blessed be He, from the Cruelty Attribute into the Compassion Attribute.

[144] Gen. R. 44:5; Cant. R. 1:14, and see also ibid., R. Berekiah's statement: *'A bag of myrrh (ṣeror ha-mor) is my Be-* *loved unto me'* (Cant. 1:13)—Said the Congregation of Israel before the Holy One, blessed be He: When You *torment me (meṣar li)*, (and) *You treat me bitterly (memar li)*, You become my *Beloved*, on the lookout for some great man in my midst, who will be able to say to the Justice Attribute: Enough now!

[145] Gen. R. 56:5; Yalkut, #101 and Yalkut, Nahum, #561.

in the days of Jeremiah Israel removed themselves (from God), the Holy One, blessed be He, said to them: What do you think? That these knots are permanent? 'That forever ('ad) the sirim are tied hand and foot' (Nahum 1:10), that forever the sarim, the Princes, are tied hand and foot? Oh no! 'But when (Israel) are drunken, untied' (ibid.), the ropes around the Princes are loosed! (Then Israel) 'are devoured as stubble full dry (ibid.)." There are no merits in perpetuity on high without continuing good action below. Hence, he who cannot find favor through the acts of Torah cannot find favor through the Akedah either.[146] The Akedah has no quarrel with Torah and the commandments, and it has not come to put an end to them or to diminish them. The very reverse! The Akedah Merit proclaims and promises that the very grace of the Fathers lies in this: the sum of the righteousness of the Fathers is there to add to and complete the reward of sons[147] who engage actively in Torah; and thereby redemption makes haste to come.

To put it briefly: Both differentiae and parallels in the two traditions on the one bound and the one crucified seem to point rather to a common source in the ancient pagan world. What survived from the heritage of idolatry which in Judaism remained peripheral grew to become dominant in the Christian world, which sought to shape and glorify the Golgotha Event in the Akedah image and like-

---

[146] Cf. above, n. 24.

[147] Cf. B. Yoma 87a: How fortunate the righteous are! Not enough that for themselves they achieve merit, but they produce merit for their children and children's children, to the end of all generations. See also J. Sanhedrin 10, 27b; Lev. R., ch. 36: Had the Patriarchs demanded immediate reward for the mitsvot they carried out in this world, where would there be the investment of merit continuing for their descendants after them? See also ibid. on the subject: "How long does the merit of the Fathers endure?" and the statement of R. Berekiah's ad Isa. 54:10, "But My love shall not depart from thee, neither shall My covenant of peace," etc. Cf. also B. Shabbat 55a, and Rabbenu Tam in Tosafot, ibid., s.v., But Samuel says: "The merit of the Fathers has been exhausted."

ness. And when Christianity placed at the center of its religion belief in the atoning power of the blood of its messiah, in Israel a need was increasingly felt to blur more and more the remnants of similar ancient beliefs from pagan times, leaving behind therefore only faint traces[148] in our sources. Withal, however, it is possible to find sup-

[148] For example, the Christians are drawn to Psalm 8: "Thou hast made him but little lower than Elohim. . . . Thou hast put all things under his feet"; note, e.g., I Corinthians 15:27. Even in a number of our old sources, signs remain of the psalm having been given an Akedah interpretation; see T. Sotah 6:5: R. Simeon ben Menasia (*aliter*, R. Simeon ben Eleazar; and so too Yalkut Makiri, Psalms, p. 49): This psalm speaks of nothing other than Isaac ben Abraham in connection with the Akedah. Cf. also Midrash Shir ha-Shirim Zuta, ed. Buber, p. 9: Two songs the ministering angels recited: one at Isaac's Akedah, "O Lord, our Lord, How glorious is Thy Name in all the earth!" etc. So too Yalkut Makiri, Psalms, p. 48. Note too Tanhuma, Wa-Yera, 18: When the Holy One, blessed be He, sought to create the world, the ministering angels said to Him: "What is man that Thou art mindful of him?" etc. He said to them, In time to come you will yet see a father slaying his son, and the son being slain, for the Sanctification of My Name. Cf. also Midrash Wa-Yosha, p. 38: "And Abraham stretched forth his hand, and took the knife to slay his son" (Gen. 22:10)— Said the Holy One, blessed be He, to the ministering angels: Have you observed My beloved Abraham, how he is proclaiming the Unity of My Name in the world? Had I listened to you when you said (so read!) at the Creation of My world, "What is man that Thou art mindful of him," etc., who would have proclaimed the Unity of My Name in this world? Note too the Midrash cited by Yalkut, #96: The Holy One, blessed be He, said to the ministering angels: Had I listened to you . . . would there be an Abraham revealing My Splendor in the world? Said the *Justice Attribute* before the Holy One, blessed be He: All those (other nine) trials You put him through, affected only his possessions; put him bodily to the test! Said the Attribute to Him: Let him sacrifice his son before You. Forthwith He said to him: "Take now thy son" (Gen. 22:2). Cf. also Bereshit Rabbati, ed. Albeck, pp. 85ff., to the effect that the ministering angels grew jealous of Abraham, because the Holy One, blessed be He, "kept consulting him over every single thing, as it is said (Gen. 18:17), 'Shall I hide from Abraham' (etc.)"—but would not consult them. "Then the ministering angels spun out accusations, saying: Very well, then, we'll leave Thy Glory and Sovereignty alone, and acclaim Abraham, Blessed be Abraham! Said the Holy One, blessed be He: Whoever honors Abraham, honors Me. And so too it says (I Sam. 2:30), 'For them that honor Me, I will honor, and they that dishonor Me shall be lightly esteemed'; and it says (Ps. 8:6), 'And Thou hast made him but little lower than Elohim.' R. Judah says: That night the Holy One, blessed be He, put

port for every one of the details of the Haggadah on the slaughter
and resurrection of Isaac in the documents of talmudic-midrashic
literature itself, independently of ideas or sources from the realm of
Christianity.

Is this to say that the Christians learned their lessons from
Judaism and the Jews picked up nothing from their Christian sur-
roundings? Not at all! Beliefs and opinions float from place to place
and pass over from one religion to another wittingly and unwittingly.
There are conceptions like the Akedah Merit that start out at first
to act as influence and end up being influenced themselves. And it
also happens that in time, owing to forgetfulness, traditions get lost,
and the loss is recovered through contact with an alien culture.

Consider one example of many. The prophet refers to "plants of
pleasantness" (Isa. 17:10). It was an old Canaanite custom to raise,
in flower pots or baskets filled with earth, tender plants which in
a few days budded and withered away speedily. Such were either
set in the field or cast into water, apparently as a charm to en-
courage a year of plenty and the blessing of rain. These are the
"gardens of Adonis" [149] in honor of the god Adonis, known abun-
dantly from Greek and Roman literature from the days of Plato to
the sixteenth century. In our sources also, in Geonic Responsa,[150]

---

him to the test by means of his son, as it
is written (Gen. 22:1), 'And God put
Abraham to the test.' "

Similar haggadot were first told in
regard to Adam, for example, that the
ministering angels mistook him and
sought to recite before him *Sanctus*,
because he filled (the frame of) the
whole world; cf. Gen. R. 8:10 and Kohelet
Zuta, p. 107; cf. Ginzberg, *Legends*, V,
86, n. 37.

[149] Ἀδώνιδος κῆποι: H. Sulze, in *Angelos*,
II (1926), 44ff., III (1928), 72ff.; ap-

parently the first so to interpret Isa.
17:10 was W. R. Smith, *Religion of the
Semites* (1899), p. 197 n.; cf. Baudissin,
Adonis und Esmun, pp. 87ff.; R. de Vaux,
"Sur quelques rapports entre Adonis et
Osiris" (*Revue Biblique*, XLII (1933),
33ff.). Cf. also Joseph Klausner, "Niteei
Naamanim," in *Alexander Ziskind Rabi-
nowitz Memorial Volume* (Tel Aviv,
1924), pp. 10-14.

[150] Simhah Asaf, *Teshuvot ha-Geonim
mi-tok ha-Genizah* (Jerusalem, 1928),
p. 155, and *Ozar ha-Geonim*, Shabbat,

signs of that custom have been preserved: "About twenty or fifteen days before Rosh ha-Shanah, you weave a number of baskets, and have a basket for each and every child of the household. You fill it with earth and manure; plant in the baskets seeds of wheat, barley, and Egyptian peas or various kinds of beans. This is called *parpisa*. . . . The seeds grow about one or two handbreadths high. Every one of the children then takes a basket and swings it round and round the head seven times and recites: This instead of me, this is my proxy, this is my substitute—and then casts it into the river."

This custom survives even today among Mediterranean peoples, especially in Southern Italy and France; here too, about twenty or fifteen days before Easter (in other regions, before the new year), they make a practice of growing wheat or barley, or one or another kind of beans, they decorate the plates or little baskets of plants, and set them up in their churches.[151] The Jews of Italy do likewise, and between Rosh ha-Shanah and Yom Kippur set the plants on their tables.[152] The specific details of such conduct demonstrate that the Jews have obviously gotten the habit anew from their neighbors, perhaps because they vaguely recalled some practice like it in their native tradition and in the old ancestral heritage. In exile, generations of Israel completely forgot the pagan Canaanite inheritance, and it was the peoples of Christendom who retrieved it for them from oblivion.

Is it possible that the like occurred with some Akedah tradi-

p. 20; cf. ibid., p. 82: Rashi's commentary in B. Shabbat 81b: *Parpisa;* cf. I. Loew, *Flora der Juden,* IV (1934), 336f. And see V. Aptowitzer in *Ha-Zofeh le-Hokmat Yisrael,* VII, p. 93, and J. Z. Lauterbach, Tashlik, *HUCA,* XI (1936), 277.

[151] Walter Baumgartner, "Das Nachleben der Adonisgärten auf Sardinien und im übrigen Mittelmeergebiet," *Schweierische Archiv für Volkskunde,* XLIII (1946), 122-148 [now reprinted in his *Zum Alten Testament und seiner Umwelt,* pp. 247-273].

[152] Aldo Neppi Modena, "I 'Giardini di Adone' in una usanza degli Ebrei d'Italia?" *Bilychnis* (Rome), Sept. 1923, pp. 85-93.

tions?[158] And may it be that in the Middle Ages the Jews recovered once again from the Christians something of the ancient pagan world which had been forgotten or suppressed?

[158] Perhaps this may serve to explain the reappearance and revival of haggadot—which, tō be sure, in almost all details can be explained by ancient midrashic sources, but which in the course of time either disappeared or were put out of sight, and the very recollection of them was lost, and in the Christian environment of the Middle Ages rose again to the surface and in full light. Note the Midrash found by R. *Isaac bar Asher* (see above, Prologue, n. 18), and the haggadah in *Shibbole ha-Leket* (above, ch. IV, n. 17), and perhaps also the midrash on Ps. 8 on the Akedah theme in Bereshit Rabbati (above, n. 148). In any event, this would be only an auxiliary cause; the basic cause is still to be sought in the Jewish experience during the Middle Ages. See below, ch. X.

X

The view of the Akedah chapter is that the one who puts to the test and commands the Akedah is God (Elohim), and the one who prevents it and makes the (subsequent) promise is the angel of the Lord (YHWH).[1]

The Sages said: Wherever in Scripture *Lord* (*YHWH*) is used, the reference is to the Mercy Attribute, as it is said (Exod. 34:6), "The Lord (*YHWH*)! the Lord! a God compassionate and gracious"; wherever *God* (*Elohim*) is used, the reference is to the Justice Attribute, as it is said (Exod. 22:8), "The case of both parties shall come before God (*Elohim*)."[2] This is what those two outstanding men, R. Yohanan and Resh Lakish, taught: the one in connection with the Akedah—*Adonai-yireh*, Lord, take note (Gen. 22:14)[3]— and the other in connection with the shofar-sounding on Rosh ha-Shanah—The Lord, amidst the sound of the shofar (Ps. 47:6).[4]

Of course, generations of readers did not overlook the alternation of the terms for deity in the biblical Akedah narrative, that in the first part *Elohim*, God, appears five times, and in the later part *YHWH*, Lord, appears five times. And in the centuries when Midrash was at its height, they spoke of the rising from the Justice Throne over to the Mercy Throne, and of turning the Punishment

---

[1] Nahmanides in his commentary *ad* Gen. 22:12.

[2] Sifre, Deut., 27; see also the statement by R. Samuel bar Nahman: Gen. R. 33:3 and 73:3.

[3] Gen. R. 56:10. See above, ch. IX, nn. 49-52.

[4] Pesikta Kahana 151b. See above, ch. IX, n. 56.

Attribute into the Rewarding Attribute. Then schools of theologians and philosophers discussed the matter and put forward definitions to purge concepts of the customary misleading figures of speech and coarse anthropomorphic expression; or they sought to solve the difficult problem of the presence of evil in the world of a good and beneficent God. For their part, the adepts at the occult drew up, from teachings about Creation out of the Primal Nothingness, notions of light and darkness, right side and left side, male and female, might and mercy. This is how Scripture was studied and taught generation after generation for centuries.

Finally, in the eighteenth century, there arose a generation who laid the foundations for biblical higher criticism, and attempted to offer a new commentary—the interpretation of people of Western culture—on the old problem of different names for God in the Holy Scriptures. Astruc,[5] one of the founding fathers of the Documentary Hypothesis, proposed that before the editor of the Book of Genesis lay two prime documents and a number of fragmentary secondary ones; hence the contradictions and disorder in Scripture, which in the seventeenth century had led the pioneers of critical study of the Bible to deny that the books of the Torah were composed by Moses.[6] In the Akedah narrative as well, Astruc discovered Document A (Gen. 22:1-10) and Document B (22:11-19).[7] Before long, and the century had not yet run out, there were biblical scholars proposing corrections and emendations of texts and documents, so that in one series there would always be *God* and in the

---

[5] [J. Astruc,] *Conjectures sur les Memoires Originaux Dont il paroit que Moyse s'est servir pour composer le Livre de la Genese* (Brussels, 1753).

[6] Astruc, pp. 422ff., mentions the following: Hobbes, *Leviathan* (1651); Isaac de la Peyrere, *Systema theologicum ex Praedamitarum hypothesi* (1655); Spinoza, *Tractatus theologico-politicus* (1670); Le Clerc, *Sentiments de quelques théologiens de Hollande* (1685); the last-mentioned retracted in his work, *De scriptore Pentateuchi* (1693).

[7] Astruc, op. cit., pp. 109-113.

other always *Lord*.[8] It did not take long before fingerprints of a
redactor or compiler were discovered who strove to unite the two
documents—and that is why he was compelled to put words into
the mouth of the angel "a *second time* from heaven" (Gen. 22:15).[9]
From this point on, critics maintained that they could distinguish
in the Akedah narrative the work of three authors. There was the
author of "The Document of God," and the author of "The Document of the Lord," and the editor-author known as *the Redactor*.[10]
Some disagreement on details remained—Critic A declaring this
verse corrupt, and Critic B doctoring that verse to relocate it from
document to document. Nevertheless no essential change of method
occurred, particularly during the decades when the Wellhausen
school was dominant.[11] For the most part it was agreed that the core

[8] Johann Gottfried Eichhorn, *Einleitung
in das Alte Testament*[3] (Reuthlingen,
1790), II, p. 310: Gen. 22:12 "vielleicht
auch יהוה zu lesen."

[9] Karl David Ilgen, *Die Urkunden des
Jerusalemischen Tempelarchivs in ihrer
Urgestalt* (Halle, 1798), p. 143: "die
Worte: *das zweyte Mahl* sind ein Zusatz
eines Sammlers, der die Reden beyder
Urkunden nicht anders zu vereinigen
wusste, als dass er zwey Mahl reden
liess." He suggests emending verse 11
to read: angel of *God* (*Elohim*), and
verse 14, *Elohim-yireh*. And in their
emendations most of the modern critics
follow him. See C. A. Simpson, *The
Early Traditions of Israel* (Oxford, 1948),
p. 83.

[10] Ilgen gave the following names to the
authors of the Documents: Authors *Eliel*
I and II, and Author *Elyah*, and a similar
distinction was made also by Hermann
Hupfeld, *Die Quellen der Genesis und
die Art ihrer Zusammensetzung* (Berlin,
1853), p. 56: $E_1E_2 = EP$, as they later

came to be signified. He regards Gen.
22: 15-18 as a redactoral addition.

[11] J. Wellhausen, "Die Composition des
Hexateuchs," *Jahrbuch für deutsche
Theologie*, XXI (1876), 409 = [3]Berlin,
1899, p. 18: Gn 22, 15-18 "ein Zusatz,
erkenntlich schon an dem שנית welches
an Jos 5:2 שנית erinnert." See the
interpretation of Josh. 5:2 by the talmudic Sages: R. *Ishmael* says: Did uncircumcised hear the voice of the Holy
One, blessed be He, at Mount Sinai?
God forbid! Circumcised they were, but
they had had no *peri'ah* (exposure of
the glans) . . . That is why the Holy
One, blessed be He, said to Joshua, Go
circumcise them *a second time*. PRE,
ch. 29, and cf. B. Yebamot 71b: Rabbah
bar Isaac said in Rab's name: Father
Abraham was not given the commandment regarding *peri'ah*, for it is said
(Josh. 5:2), 'Circumcise again the children of Israel *the second time*. See also
Cant. R. 1:12 and 3:6: "Threescore
mighty men"—The Sages interpret the

of the Akedah narrative (Gen. 22:1-13, 19) was established by the
Elohist narrator, into which a Yahwist interpolater or editor inserted
additions (vv. 14-18).[12] True, at the present time the assumptions of
this school have been seriously challenged, or at least its certainties
have become maybes; and again there are commentators who say
that the whole Akedah chapter, despite the different names for the
divine, comes from the hands of one author.[13]

Once again explanations of the different terms for deity are
renewed. *God* refers to the one who demands human sacrifice, "who
puts to the test and commands the Akedah," and *Lord* to "the one
who prevents it and makes the (subsequent) promise,"[14] who takes
pity on man and forbids sacrificing him.[15] We are back, then, to the
original problem: are there perhaps before us two distinct religious
layers, one from the stratum of ancient idolatry where the sacrifice
of human first born was practised, and the other from biblical
religion which put an end to this cruel practice and substituted
animal sacrifice?[16]

---

verse as a reference to the ones coming
out of Egypt, the sixty myriads, "the
ones handling the sword" . . . Who circumcised them? R. *Berekiah* said, Moses
did the circumcising, Aaron the *peri'ah*,
and Joshua served the drink. Some say:
Joshua did the circumcising, Aaron the
peri'ah, and Moses served the drink,
even as it is said, "Circumcise again the
children of Israel *the second time.*" And
why a second time? Evidently he had
circumcised them *the first time.*

[12] Fr. Tuch, *Commentar über die Genesis*
(1838;[2] 1871): Gn 22, 1-13, 19 Grund-
schrift; 22, 14-18 Ergänzer ("in gewohnter
Weise: שׂנית!"); A. Dillmann, *Genesis*[3]
(1875): Gn 22, 1-13, 19 = E; Gn 22,
14-18 = J. See also Julian Morgenstern,
A Jewish Interpretation of the Book of
Genesis (Cincinnati, 1920), p. 164. J.
Skinner, *Genesis* (1910), p. 331. Others
mark the verses Gen. 22: 15-18 as an
addition: H. Gunkel, *Genesis*[4] (1917), p.
239; O. Procksch, *Genesis* (1924).

[13] Paul Volz, *Der Elohist als Erzähler, ein*
Irrweg der Pentateuchkritik (Giessen,
1933), pp. 40ff.

[14] See above, n. 1.

[15] Knobel, *Kommentar zur Genesis* (1852),
and especially Umberto Cassuto, *La*
questione della Genesi (Florence, 1934),
p. 52; see also Martin Buber, "Genesis-
probleme," *MGWJ*, LXXX (1936), 85f.

[16] P. von Bohlen, *Die Genesis historisch-*
kritisch erläutert (Königsberg, 1835), p.
231 (cf. Fr. Tuch, *Comm. Genesis*[2], 1871,
pp. 337ff.).

Indeed, there have even been attempts to separate two distinct stories in the Akedah chapter: the account of Isaac who was slain and burned on his pyre, and that other version according to which Isaac was saved and a ram was offered up in his place.[17] From the earlier story (vv. 1-5, 9, 15-19) we lack the report of the act of sacrifice, the description of the slaughter of the son; but the end of the story, the Lord blessing the father, has survived: "Because *you have done* this," "because *you have obeyed* My command," "I will bestow My blessing upon you," etc. And nothing in the chapter's text is to be changed, except for the one Hebrew word *shenit*, "a second time" (v. 15), which does not belong to the original of the earlier story—and was very likely added only after verses 11 and 12 were interpolated in the chapter, two verses which are no more than an expansion of what is reported in verse 13, which belongs to the corpus of the second story (vv. 6-8, 10, 13, 14) devoted to the saving of Isaac, and the ram as proxy sacrifice. In this second story there was no mention at all of an angel calling from on high, exactly as verse 13 suggests: for had Abraham been taken by surprise and been prodded "from heaven," his eye would already have been lifted upward, and there would have been no place for "And Abraham *lifted* his eyes" (of verse 13). But verses 11 and 12 were inserted as a kind of explanation that, when suddenly chance provided Abraham with a ram, through his mind flashed the idea of offering the animal in place of his son, for he discerned the finger of God in the coincidence: he thought to himself, Surely this is *an angel* come on a mission from the Holy One, blessed be He, to provide me with this ram in place of my son![18] In the original source, however, the angel spoke no more than one time—in the

---

[17] Micha Josef Bin Gorion, *Sinai und Garizim* (Berlin, 1926), pp. 121ff. This is the Hebrew writer Michah Yosef Berdichevski; see also his *Me-Ozar ha-Aggadah*, I (Berlin, 1914), pp. 52-60.

[18] Cf. Rashbam and Sforno *ad loc.*

earlier story, when he promised blessings on the father who had slain his son. Erase from verse 15, therefore, that superfluous addition, "a second time." [19]

The ancients, of course, never permitted themselves the liberty of laying their hands on verses they did not know how to interpret, and it never entered their minds to scrape away or scratch out anything in the received text. But they were no less sensitive to difficulties and tried to remove them in their own way, by reconciling the verses as they were, either by what appeared to them to be *peshat*, literal exegesis, or by way of *derash*, imaginative, homiletical exegesis, which they loved so much.

The talmudic Sages, it will be found, were also perplexed: Why two calls from heaven? And as is their reverent way, they replied: "Then an angel called to him" (Gen. 22:11). Said Abraham to him: Who are you? He replied, I'm an angel. Said Abraham to him, When He told me, "Now, take your son," the Holy One, blessed be He, Himself spoke to me; and if there is anything (else) He now wants, let Him tell me! Immediately "the angel of the Lord called to Abraham a second time" (22:15). Why *a second time*? *Because Abraham refused to listen on the first one.* [20] "Abraham said to the angel: The Holy One, blessed be He, told me to slay him, and you tell me not to slay him. If the master instructs one way and the disciple instructs another, whose instructions does one listen to? [21] Forthwith the Holy One, blessed be He, opened up the

[19] Bin Gorion, *Sinai und Garizim*, p. 128, also alludes to Joshua 5:2. Cf. Bereshit Rabbati, p. 191, and above, n. 11.

[20] Tanhuma, Wa-Yera, 23 and Tanhuma, ed. Buber, 46, I, 114f., end; and cf. Yelamdenu in Yalkut Talmud Torah, Mann, p. 308.

[21] Midrash Wa-Yosha, p. 38. And note Abrabanel's commentary *ad* Gen. 22:15: And in Gen. R. it is said that Abraham said, Is there such a thing as a *slave protesting against his master's command*? Your Master said: "And offer him there as a burnt offering," and you say, "And don't do a thing to him." As for me, that is an impossible state of affairs, "*Adonai-yireh*, Let the Lord look to," and not the angel. That is why it is said *a second time*. Cf. Midrash Aggadah, ed. Buber, p. 52: "'And he said, Don't lay your hand.' Said Abraham to him: Maybe

firmament and deep darkness, 'and He said, By Myself I swear, saith the Lord' " (22:16).[22]

Others put another complexion on the matter: " 'A second time from heaven,' for the original revelation was interrupted, and this was the second revelation." [23] And perhaps this view is in accordance with that rabbinic comment, that only in connection with Moses was there no interruption of the Holy Spirit: "He would cease speaking to every other prophet, but never so long as Moses was alive did He cease (to speak with him)." [24]

As for the medieval commentators, some combined verses 14 and 15 and went to great lengths in their solution: "The *peshat*, the literal interpretation is this—*Adonai-yireh, the Lord will note* what the world will say of me, *this day on the mount of the Lord will be seen* if Abraham is so righteous after all, if he will slay his son for the sake of the Holy One, blessed be He, who commanded the slaying. And when they see that I have *not* sacrificed him, they will say that I transgressed Thy commands and that I do not keep

---

you're Satan and you're seeking to deceive me. Said the angel to him: No; on the contrary, I am *the emissary of the Holy One, blessed be He, who takes no pleasure in human sacrifice."* See Bereshit Rabbati, p. 90: "And don't do a thing to him" (Gen. 22:12). Said Abraham to him, Who are you? The angel: An emissary of the Master of the universe. Abraham: Maybe you're Satan and you seek to trick me into transgressing my Creator's will? Angel: I am the one who announced to you the birth of this son, I am the one who said to you (Gen. 18:10), "I will return, return, to you." Why this "return" twice? Once, to tell of his birth, and once for his deliverance. And now I've been appointed *paraclete* to save your only son. And

this is the reason Abraham recognized that he was an emissary of the Master of the universe. And in *Pardes,* in the Selections, 44, ed. Ehrenreich, p. 93: "I will surely return to you." But nowhere do we find that the angel returned to bring the good tidings to Abraham. However, he here promised him "I will surely return," for that lad will be in need of life. And when was that? At Mount Moriah.

[22] See above, n. 20.

[23] Midrash Ner ha-Sekalim; cf. M. M. Kasher, *Torah Shelemah*, p. 908, #179.

[24] Exod. R., ch. 2. And note Midrash Aggadah, p. 53: Hence, the Shekinah did not speak with him a third time. Cf. Bereshit Rabbati, p. 191.

Thy commandments except when it is to my advantage. And that slander which they spread about me, *Adonai-yireh*, Lord, take note, it is all lies." [25]

Along such lines commentators still continued in the generation of the banishment from Spain: *"Because he did not complete the act* which he had every intention of doing, and feared lest it would not be regarded as though he had carried it out, he named that place in accordance with what he had intended to do; and the meaning of *Adonai-yireh* is, Lord, take note of what I contemplated and said I would do, if the angel had not prevented me. Howbeit, let the good intention and integrity of my heart *be manifest today on the mount of the Lord* before the world. . . . And that is why the word of the angel came to him *a second time.* . . . Abraham attained this great honor *as though he had actually carried out the act."* [26] Seems as though in these words you hear an echo of an ancient reproof, that Father Abraham did not consummate his act. The fact is that this idea recurs again and again in the Christian

---

[25] *Hadar Zekenim* 8a. And similarly, *Daat Zekenim* 11a: *"Adonai-yireh, Lord, take note* that it is my wish and desire to slay my son as He commanded me; *hence the saying nowadays:* I know that nowadays it will be said, the deceit of human beings *will be seen in the mountain of the Lord:* Will even a godfearing man like Abraham sacrifice his son in accordance with the Rock's command? And when they see us returning, they will say that I did not want to carry out the Lord's commandment. But then *it will be seen* that the restraint is not on my part." The first so to interpret the verse, it would seem, was R. Hezekiah bar Manoah; see *Hizkuni* on the Pentateuch (Lwow, 1859), Wa-Yera, end: *"Adonai-yireh*—so Abraham speaks: Let

the Lord take note and be my Witness, that I have done what He commanded. For I know that in a number of places *it will be said today, in the mountain of the Lord* whither Abraham led his son, it will become manifest to us whether he is capable of honoring Him and of slaying his son. And when they see my son returning with me, they will say that I proved the liar to God on high and despised His words, and they will not believe that the cause was the Lord's. Then let the Holy One, blessed be He, *take note* that I have not rebelled against His commands and may He be my Witness." Cf. Azulai's *Shem ha-Gedolim*, book section, s.v. *Hizkuni.*

[26] Isaac ben Aramah, *Akedat Yizhak*, Wa-Yera pericope (end).

environment: "And Abraham cried to his God. . . . Let now Thy mercy note well what all manner of men will say *this day*, namely, *that I did not sacrifice my son*, and that all of my intention was vain and a lie. . . . And the whole purpose of Abraham's prayer and supplication was that God would not prevent him from offering up Isaac as a sacrifice even *after* (*the sacrifice of*) *the ram*, for otherwise his intention and wish to serve God would not be believed. For this reason the *second order* came to him from the angel, who said to him: 'Because you have done this, and have not withheld your son, your favored one'—*because you persist and always seek to offer him up as a burnt offering*, therefore, as a reward the Lord swears 'that I will surely bless you,' etc. That is why the second order came from the angel, and the angel did not include this in the first order." [27]

So Scripture triumphed after all—but was it a triumph? The ancient pagan demand for actual sacrifice of children was not uprooted from the world, nor perhaps from the heart either. The ancient argument was not silenced, that at the Akedah there had been *no* consummation of the act. Such words had been heard long before, in Alexandria in Philo's time,[28] in Palestine in the time of the Hadrianic persecutions,[29] and subsequently in many countries, particularly in Christian kingdoms, in the Middle Ages, when the taunt was frequently directed against Israel that the Akedah was no sacrifice in truth, but only a hint of what was to come, the completed act in the days of Jesus.[30]

Indeed, there may already be something of this spiritual climate in R. Ephraim of Bonn's *Akedah*, which is here being published for the first time. This poem contains a new interpretation of the

[27] Don Isaac Abrabanel's Pentateuch Commentary (Hanau, 1710), *ad loc.*

[28] See above, ch. I.

[29] Above, ch. II.

[30] Ch. IX, nn. 17-28.

Scriptural passage and an answer to the Sages' question: What purpose is served by this call "a second time from heaven"? This was Rabbi Ephraim's solution and song: that Abraham did exactly as he had been commanded, and immediately slew Isaac *one time*:

> *Down upon him fell the resurrecting dew, and he revived.*
> *(The father) seized him (then) to slaughter him once more.*
> *Scripture, bear witness! Well-grounded is the fact:*
> And the Lord called Abraham, even a second time from heaven.

.   .   .   .

> *He was swept by the flood of celestial tears*
> Into Eden, the garden of God.

That is to say, had it not been for the flood of tears the ministering angels shed, which swept over Isaac and carried him off the top of the altar and bore him to the Garden of Eden, his father would have slain him a *second* time! Let the whole wide world know to what lengths fear of Heaven reaches—the father was ready to slay his son, his favored one, not once *but twice*, so that His Glorious and Awesome Name might be sanctified in the world.

Rabbi Ephraim drew upon haggadic traditions which told of Isaac's soul—that it had taken wing but that the Holy One, blessed be He, had restored it to him by means of the dew of resurrection;[81] thus Isaac learned that in the future this is how the dead would come to life again; whereupon he burst forth with: Blessed be He who quickens the dead.[82] Isaiah 33, the ancient *haftarah*, the prophetic reading for the Torah reading of the Akedah pericope, joins

---

[81] Lekah Tob, p. 161. The Midrash *Lekah Tob* was known to R. Ephraim, and he mentions it in his *Sefer Zekirah* (NS, p. 65, end = Habermann, p. 123).

[82] PRE, ch. 31.

the Akedah to the cry of Ariels, "the angels of peace weeping bitterly," and the tears of these holy ones kept falling until Abraham's knife melted away.[33] Rabbi Isaac ben Asher ha-Levi found a midrash to the effect "that Isaac was secreted in Paradise for two years in order to be healed from the incision made in him by his father when he began to offer him up as a sacrifice." [34] Out of these haggadic elements was composed the story of the flood of tears from on high, which flowed like a stream and swept Isaac into the Garden of Eden. But this *second* slaying, which Abraham attempted against Isaac, where did Rabbi Ephraim get it from? "Scripture, bear witness! well-grounded is the fact: And the Lord called Abraham, even *a second time* from heaven." Was this terrifying thought born only from meticulous study of the biblical text? Or is it perhaps an echo out of the historical nightmare of those times?

We have already referred to the poems and chronicles which report the conduct of the Mainz martyrs of 1096,[35] that they slew one another inside the bishop's palace, when "the vagabonds," that is, the Crusaders, captured the gate of the fortress and penetrated into the courtyard; and there was no escape any longer for Jews save by conversion. The Mainz community elected to be slain for the Sanctification of the Name, as is written in the documents of those times. Now, also recorded in "The Account of Old Disasters" and in the memoirs of R. Solomon bar Samson as well, is the sequel of the story of the Mainz saints: "And after that the children of the holy covenant who were inside were slain, the uncircumcised came upon them to strip the corpses and sweep them out of the rooms; and they threw the naked bodies out of the windows, heaps and heaps, and piles on piles, until these formed a high mountain

---

[33] Gen. R. 56:5 and 7.   [35] Above, ch. III, nn. 5f.
[34] See above, Prologue, n. 18.

as it were. Many victims were still alive when they were being
hurled out, and there was still some breath of life left in them. With
their fingers these victims made signs: A little water, please. When
the vagabonds observed this, that there was still some life to them,
they kept asking them: Do you want to defile yourselves? We'll
let you have water to drink and you may still be saved! But the
victims shook their heads and looked up to their Father in heaven,
as though to say: No! And with their fingers they kept pointing to
the Holy One, blessed be He. And because of all their wounds they
could not utter a word. So they proceeded to torture them some
more, until, *they killed them a second time.*" [80]

In these memoirs it is also told—and so too in R. Eliezer bar
Nathan's Book of the Disasters of 1096—of the community of
Mehr,[37] a village on the Rhine, that the prince of the city handed
the Jews over to the Crusaders, who "slew some of them; those
whom they left alive they forcibly befouled, doing with them as
they pleased. One saint—Master Shemariah was his name—fled
from there together with his wife and three sons, because the
bishop's bursar promised them that for a high price, which Shemariah paid, the bursar would get him away and save him. The
bursar led them here and there, detained them in one place after
another, and kept pressing for more money. So Master Shemariah
sent to his sons in Speyer for more money. His sons sent him a
mark of gold. Once the bursar got his hands on the money, he
brought them and turned them over to the enemy in the village of
Tremonia.[38] When Master Shemariah got there, the citizens of the
town rejoiced greatly over him because they knew him. They agreed
to wait until the morrow and to do what they wished. In great joy
they held a feast, and the family of Shemariah ate with them—but

[80] NS, p. 14, and cf. ibid., p. 55 = Habermann, p. 39, and cf. ibid., p. 102.
[37] Mehr (cf. Salfeld, p. 419).
[38] Tremonia = Dortmund.

observing the religious requirements for proper and clean food, and (eating) with previously unused utensils; for they said to the villagers: So long as we are in our old faith, we would like to act as we have been accustomed to do up to now; tomorrow we will all be one. Tonight put us into one room, until tomorrow, because we are tired and worn out from the difficult journey. So the townspeople did. Then while it was still night, Master Shemariah arose, and girding himself with might he slaughtered his wife and three sons; and then he put the knife into himself. He fell unconscious, but was still not dead. On the following morning when the enemy came upon him . . . they found him lying on the ground. They asked him: Do you want to convert from your faith to ours?—because you still have a possibility to go on living. But he answered them: God forbid that I should forswear the Living God. . . . So the townspeople dug a grave, and he, R. Shemariah the saint, walked up to and into it by himself; he took his three sons and laid them to the left side, his wife to the right side, and himself in the middle. Then the people began to throw on him the earth from the graveside. And all that day, till the following morn, he kept crying out loud and weeping, and keened over himself, his sons, his helpmeet lying beside him. Then the enemies of the Lord came *a second time* and removed him, still alive, from the grave, so that he might recant and confess their error. Again they asked him: Do you want to give up your God? But that saint R. Shemariah refused to barter the Great and the Glorious for the cheap, and he held fast to his integrity till his last breath. So they put him into the grave *a second time* and threw earth upon him, and there the saint died for the Unity of the Glorious and Awesome Name, and there he remained steadfast in his trial like *Father Abraham*. O how fortunate he was, O his fortunate lot!" [39]

[39] NS, pp. 23-24 and p. 44 = Habermann, pp. 51-52, 79-80.

Here, then, the writer of the memoirs explains from whom it was
that the heroes who did His will in the Rhine region learned their
lesson: from the haggadic lore about the sacrificer and the sacrifice
on Mount Moriah. Indeed, there are times your imagination has it
that perhaps the Midrashim on the Akedah theme and the Akedah
poems themselves also speak of contemporary events; and maybe
even the biblical figures were drawn in the light of the actualities
of the Crusades, when the saints of Germany and France sanctified
the Name in droves.

In the Book of the Disasters of 1096 by R. Eliezer bar Nathan it
is reported that "the enemy in common council decided to torment
the saints of Elnere[40] with tortures until these capitulated to their
defilement. The Jews got wind of this decision, and all of them
assembled in one hall. They recited their confessionals before their
Creator. Then the saints volunteered to slaughter them all, for in
that city there were about three hundred souls. . . . With the
doors shut, the saints took hold of their swords and slaughtered
them all. . . . Of all those souls no more than two young men
and two infants remained alive, and even they *had had their throats
cut, but continued to live.*" [41]

The midrash that Isaac had had his throat cut but was healed
"from the incision his father made in him when he began to slaughter
him" [42]—what is its date? R. Isaac bar Asher found that midrash;
and, who knows? perhaps the bloody events of the beginnings of
the Crusades are already reflected in it.

It is the practice of the chroniclers and the poets to describe the
great desire of these ṣaddikim, the righteous, "who yearned to
sanctify the Glorious and Awesome Name with rejoicing and good
cheer, *as a man on his way to a feast.*" [43] And so you will find in

[40] Elnere, today Eller (cf. Salfeld).

[41] NS, p. 42, cf. p. 20 = Habermann,
p. 78, and cf. pp. 46f.

[42] Cf. above n. 34.

[43] NS, p. 24, Habermann, p. 52.

the *Selihot* and *Kinot*, the Penitential poems and dirges, on the
violence and the murders in the days of the Crusaders:

> *Fathers slaughter their sons, and wallow in their blood* . . .
> *Rejoicing, they make haste to affirm the Unity of Thy Name* . . .
> *Fathers and sons together, grooms with their brides*
> *Hurry to the slaughter as to the bridal chamber.*[44]

> *Has it ever been heard or ever been seen,*
> *Who can believe so amazing a thing?*
> *As to the beautiful bridal canopy, sons are led to the slaughter—*
> *Most Highly Exalted, when such things happen, how can You hold*
>   *Your peace?*[45]

Now, we find this idiom also on the subject of the Akedah in late
Midrashim: "While Abraham was building the altar, Isaac kept
handing him the wood and the stones. Abraham was like *to a man
who builds the wedding house for his son*, and Isaac was like *to a
man getting ready for the wedding feast*, which he does with joy."[46]
And this is the "Midrash" cited by *Yalkut Shimeoni:*[47] "Both of them
brought the stones, both of them brought the fire, both of them
brought the wood. Abraham was like *him who makes a wedding
house for his son*, and Isaac was like *him who makes the wedding
feast for himself.*" Would you say that the *payyetanim*, the poets,
draw upon the Midrash as usual? Or perhaps woven into the fabric
of the Midrash is something from the vocabulary and spirit of the
medieval saints?[48]

---

[44] R. Kalonymos bar Judah in his lament
"The voice, Jacob's voice, in a moan,"
Sefer ha-Demaot, I, p. 198 = Habermann,
p. 65.

[45] R. David bar Meshullam, in the *Selihah*
"O God, do not hush up the shedding
of my blood!" H. Brody, *Mibhar ha-*

Shirah ha-Ivrit, p. 223 = Habermann,
p. 71.

[46] Midrash Wa-Yosha, p. 73.

[47] #101.

[48] Cf. the story about the *parnas* (communal leader) of the Cologne community,

So indeed R. Hillel, the brother of R. Ephraim of Bonn, also put it, regarding the martyrs of Blois: [49]

And when it was said, Bring them out to the fire,
They rejoiced together, as a bride at the bridal canopy.
"It is for us to praise," they recited, their souls filled with longing.

What these words mean is made clear by what the community of Orleans, "the city nigh to the holy martyrs," [50] wrote to Rabbenu Tam and informed him of, that thirty-two souls went up in flames in Blois: "In the morning they lit the fire. Now when the flames shot up, with one accord they let out a joyous shout and lifted their sweet voices. The Gentiles came and told us about it; and they said to us: What is this song of yours? We never heard such a sweet song. At first the victims' voices were soft, but in the end they raised their voices fortissimo and together called out, '*Alenu le-shabeah,*' 'As for us, we must praise.' And the fire burned . . . and the victims called to . . . the foe . . . and said: Behold, we're inside this fire *but it is powerless against us.* . . . So the foe put on even more coals, and still the victims were not burned up. . . . And the saints of God on High were burned, the soul on fire but the body intact. And so all the uncircumcised testify, that not one of the bodies was burned up . . ." [51]

Master Juda bar Abraham, who slew his son and daughter-in-law: "Behold now, the bridal canopy I make today for my daughter, the bride" (NS, p. 20 = Habermann, p. 47).

[49] "The perfect in faith of Israel": *Sefer ha-Demaot,* p. 231 = Habermann, p. 138.

[50] NS, p. 68 = Habermann, p. 125 (end).

[51] NS, p. 32 (and p. 68) = Habermann, p. 143 (and p. 126). It is from the Hasidim, the saintly circles of France and Germany, that "the tradition of scholars and saints" derives how a person can surrender himself to fire and sword for the Sanctification of the Name, *and feel no pain or any sensation,* so that in him is fulfilled "They have struck me, and I felt it not, they have beaten me, and I knew it not" (Prov. 23:35); cf. Samson b. Zadok, *Tashbes,* sec. 415, in the name of R. Meir of Rothenburg. So these ideas wind their way as far as Spain and find exalted expression in "The Amraphel Scroll," by R. Abraham ben Eliezer ha-Levi of the Spanish exiles. See

Where did they find their model, those martyrs of Blois? Were they already familiar with the haggadah about Isaac who, as the flames shot up, burst into song? Or was the haggadah quoted in *Sefer ha-Pardes*[52] created under the influence of the behavior of the saints and martyrs of the Middle Ages? "And this is the reason we make mention of the Fathers in the vesper Prayer, the *minhah*, of the Sabbath. . . . *Song* is the term used in connection with Isaac, because in the haggadah we find: 'Sing in the Lord, O ye righteous' (Ps. 33:1)—When the righteous behold the Shekinah of the Holy One, blessed be He, they recite the song of praise immediately. For thus we find that when Isaac was undergoing Akedah, he beheld the heavens open up; and at once he recited the song of praise. . . . Forthwith Isaac was bound *on top of the fire* . . . and he beheld above him the Shekinah in heaven standing by to receive him as sweet fragrance. Then sang out Isaac and recited the song of praise. And what is the song of praise he recited? The song which accompanies sacrifice offering."

The boundaries between midrash and reality get blurred; and it is not always easy to decide whether the haggadah in praise of the Fathers came first, or whether this haggadah was in turn influenced by the acts prompted by despair and daring of the later descendants of the Fathers in the exile of Germany and France. R. Ephraim of Bonn knew and collected the details of what was happening; and in a Book of *Memoirs*[53] wrote down the decrees and persecutions of his times. He even prepared a commentary on the Mahzor[54] and composed poems based on the massacre of saints in the time of the Crusaders.[55] While still a boy he began to soak

---

Gershom Scholem, *Chapters in the History of Kabbalah Literature* [in Hebrew] (Jerusalem, 1931), pp. 125ff. and 138.

[52] Ed. Ehrenreich, p. 316.

[53] NS, pp. 58ff. = Habermann, pp. 115ff.

[54] See above, ch. III, n. 3.

[55] Zunz, *Literaturgeschichte*, p. 290.

up traditions and reports of the fortitude of those slain for the
Sanctification of His Name. When the storm of the Second Crusade
burst, he was thirteen years old; and he and his relations fled in
1146,[56] after the Feast of Sukkot, to the fortress of Wolkenburg,
which was under the protection of the Bishop of Cologne, there to
take shelter from the fury of those who had gone wild with destruction of Jews. "And we cried out to our God and said: Ah, Lord
our God, it is not yet fifty years, a jubilee span, since our blood
was shed for the Unity of Thy Glorious Name, in a time of great
slaughter." [57] And while they waited there to be saved and redeemed,
no doubt they pondered and talked long over the praises of the
ṣaddikim and the holy congregations who "sprayed their own blood
and the blood of their dear children, and underwent many an
Akedah, and built altars, and prepared sacrifices: O God, remember
them to the good." [58] And perhaps from what his ears had picked
up while he was still of tender age, fear-ridden and impressionable,
years later when the commentator and poet tried to resolve the
difficulties in the biblical Akedah narrative, there rose to the surface,
from the hidden recesses of his soul:

> (The father) seized him (then) to slaughter him once more.
> Scripture, bear witness! Well-grounded is the fact:

if not in Scripture, then in the experience of the Jews in the Middle
Ages.

---

[56] Hence, he was born in the year 1132.
In his memoirs are recorded events up
to the year 1196. He died between 1197
and 1200. See V. Aptowitzer, Introduction to Sefer Rabiah, p. 321.

[57] NS, p. 58 (end) = Habermann, pp.
115-116.

[58] NS, p. 66 = Habermann, p. 123.

THE AKEDAH

by

Rabbi Ephraim ben Jacob of Bonn

INTRODUCTORY NOTE

The text of the *Akedah* [underlying the present translation] is based on three MSS: Oxford MS 1154, no. 205 (= A); Berlin MS 9, no. 124 (= B); Selihot MS 446, The Jewish Theological Seminary of America, no. 172 (= N). The late Professor Aaron Freiman called my attention to MS A. A copy of MS B, from the Research Institute for Hebrew Poetry in Jerusalem, came to me thanks to the late Salmann Schocken, and to members of the staff of the Institute, Mr. A. M. Habermann and the late Dr. M. Zulai, who took pains to help me. MS N was put at my disposal—as indeed all the many literary treasures which he gathered and assembled with perspicacity and great diligence—by the late Professor Alexander Marx.

The *Akedah* is made up of 26 stanzas, each one consisting of four lines, the last of which is always a biblical verse. AABB is the rhyme scheme for all the stanzas except the last, which has one rhyme for all four lines. Through stanza 12 (line 48), lines 1 and 3 of each stanza are formed with an ATBASH [as we might say in English, AZBY] acrostic. Thereafter, the poet uses the first consonant in lines 1 and 3 of the remaining stanzas for the signature EPHRAIM BAR JACOB, BE-MIGHTY IN-TORAH AND-IN-MITSVOT.

Let me recall my Fathers' (names)
  Today before Thee, examiner and knower (of hearts).
Oh grant the Fathers' merits to the sons,
  The father an old man, and the child, of his old age.

You told your favorite to offer up his only one,
  On one of the mountains to enact the priest:
'Offer Me as sacrifice the soul of him you love,
  Get it for Me, for it pleases Me well."

You called upon him to withstand the trial,
  As calls a king upon a seasoned warrior:

---

1 In the idiom of Gen. 41:9, "I must make mention today of my offenses."

2 *examiner* "The Righteous that seest the reins and the heart": Jer. 20:12.

and knower "Seeketh out my soul": Ps. 142:5 and Ruth 2:10 ("take cognizance of me").

3 B. Shabbat 55a: And why particularly the *Taw* as the sign? . . . Rabbi Johanan said: *Tahon*, Tie down (to us) graciously the Merit of the Fathers. See Saul Lieberman, *Greek in Jewish Palestine*, p. 189.

4 Gen. 44:20.

5 Sifre, Deut., 352: Six were called favorites (*yedidim*). . . . Abraham was called favorite, as it is said, "What hath My favorite to do in My house" (Jer. 11:15). And see B. Menahot 53b (top).

6 Gen. 22:2.

to enact the priest (*le-male yado*), in the idiom of Exod. 28:41; and see Pesikta R. 170a: Said the Holy One, blessed be He, to Abraham: When you arrive at the place I shall sanctify you and make you priest.

7 Gen. 22:2.

8 Judg. 14:3.

9-11 B. Sanhedrin 89b: "Take now your son" (Gen. 22:2)—R. Simeon bar Abba said: The word "now" (*na*, literally, I beg of thee, please) is nothing other than an expression for "please." A parable: It is like a king of flesh and blood who found himself with many battles on his hands. He had one *seasoned warrior* (lit., victorious hero) [Tanhuma, Wa-Yera, 22 (beginning): victorious in all battles; Yalkut, end of #96: who was victorious over them all; cf. MhG]. Once, a fierce battle raged. Said to him [the king, to that warrior, Tanhuma, ibid.], I beg of you, prove your mettle in this battle for my sake, lest they say: The previous ones were hardly anything real. So too the Holy One, blessed be He, said to Abraham: I put you to the test any number of [Tanhuma: nine] times, and in all of them you proved your mettle; now *prove it* in this *test* for My sake, lest they say: There was nothing real to the previous ones.

By this you shall be tested and prove victorious.
   The Lord trieth the righteous.

The wild ass took pride in his bleeding and brayed:
   Drops of my blood I gave at the age of thirteen!
The beloved whispered: Oh that God would take me,
   Yea, let Him take all.

Alert, (the father) ran to carry out a mitsvah,

11 *Nishan* (victorious); so vocalized in the MS.

12 Ps. 11:5, and as the talmudic Sages say, A potter does not trouble to test defective pottery, etc. What does he test? Choice pottery. . . . A flax-worker with excellent flax: the more he beats it down, the more it improves. So the Holy One, blessed be He, puts only the righteous to test. Cf. Gen. R. 32:3, 34:2, 55:2, and parallels. Similarly in the *Akedah* poem composed by R. Ephraim's contemporary and fellow townsman, R. Joel bar Isaac, "The Lord examines the righteous to gird up his loins/ . . . Like a potter the pottery testing, the hammer the kettle" (Habermann, p. 111). Similarly the poet R. Baruch of Mainz: "Never in ten tests did that *saddik* prove lax/ . . . The proof note well: the pottery and flax" (Habermann, *Yediot ha-Makon le-Heker ha-Shirah,* VI, 1945, p. 121).

13 *wild ass* Ishmael Gen. 16-12.
   brayed MS reads: *yinhak,* cf. Job 6:5.

14 *I gave* (lit., drained out, *masiti*), Lev. 1:15. And see midrashic comments, that Ishmael kept boasting and saying to Isaac: As to carrying out *mitsvot,* I am greater than you, for you were only eight days old when you were circumcised, but I was thirteen years old (B. Sanhedrin 89b,

and cf. Targum Jonathan *ad* Gen. 22:1). I am more of a *saddik* than you. . . . I felt the full pain of circumcision. . . . But at the time of your circumcision, you were only an infant, eight days old . . . you had no real knowledge of pain. . . . If you'd have been thirteen years old, you would never have accepted the pain (fragment from Yelamdenu, in L. Ginzberg, *Ginze Schechter,* I, p. 55, and Tanhuma, Wa-Yera, 18).

15 *beloved* referring to Isaac (note the expression in Gen. 22:2, "whom *you* love," and see the sources cited in the preceding note). Isaac replied to Ishmael: Don't taunt me with (your act with) *one* part of your body (B. Sanhedrin, ibid.), or with the three drops of blood you gave the Holy One, blessed be He, on credit (Tanhuma, ibid.). As for me, if He were to demand my *whole* body, I would not hold back (cf. Targum Jonathan, ibid.: If the Holy One, blessed be He, were to demand *every one of my limbs,* I would not hold back).

16 II Sam. 19:31.

17 Sifra, Tazria, 1 and B. Pesahim 4a: The alert ones rise early to carry out commandments, as it is said, "So Abraham rose early" (Gen. 22:3).

And yearned to saddle his own ass himself,
(Bound to God) by a knot of love, that outweighed dignity.
Behold, O Lord, Thou knowest it altogether.

Then came the Satan, standing close by them,
Murmuring, "Might one exchange a word with thee?"
Cried the perfect one, "I will walk in mine integrity,"
For so the King has appointed.

On the third day they arrived at Scopus,
Then to their Maker they looked:

18 "And he saddled his ass" (ibid.): Did he not have any number of servants? But for the glory of God (he did it himself) (Mekilta, Be-Shallah, 2:1; cf. Gen. R. 55:8).

19 Tannaite source, a *baraita*, in B. Sanhedrin 105b; *Tanna*, it was taught in the name of R. Simeon ben Eleazar: *Love overrides* the lines imposed by *greatness* (dignity)—Abraham is the proof of it.

knot The idiom is that of "tied in love to him" (Gen. R. 54:1 and parallels), "tie knots of hatred" (T. Sanhedrin 14:3). And perhaps our poet is being swept along by the *Akedah* of R. Kalonymos be-Rabbi Judah, which begins "Behind, a ram caught," and line 20 of which goes: "His pity he crushed, and the line did he override, though his heart went out with love to him to whose soul he was tied."

20 Ps. 139:4.

21 The Satan dogging the footsteps of Abraham and Isaac, on the model of Job 1:6 and 2:1.

22-23 The talmudic Sages related *nissah*, "put to the test," of Gen. 22:1 to *ha-*

nissah (if one try, venture, might one exchange) of Job 4:2; cf. B. Sanhedrin 89b: Satan got to the road ahead of him. He said to Abraham: "If one venture a word unto thee, wilt thou be weary?" (Job, ibid.). Said Abraham to him: "But as for me, I will walk in mine integrity" (Ps. 26:11). See MhG, p. 346 and notes, and also Midrash Composed under the Holy Spirit, p. 63, in Mann. See what I wrote above, ch. IX, on the Satan's quarrel with the Akedah.

24 Esth. 1:8.

25-28 PRE, ch. 31: On the third day they reached Scopus. . . . He saw the Glory of the Shekinah standing on top of the mountain. . . . He said to Isaac: My son, do you see anything on one of these mountains? Isaac replied: Yes . . . *a pillar* of fire reaching straight up from earth to heaven [Gen. R. 56:2: He saw *a cloud* knotted to the mountain]. Then Abraham understood that the lad was found acceptable as a whole burnt offering. Cf. the PRE version published by Michael Higger in *Horeb*, X (1948), 195.

26 In the idiom of Isa. 17:7.

The pillar of cloud shone in its splendor
  On the top of the mount, like devouring fire.

The alert one piled on his son
  Faggots for the sacrifice, for the burnt offering.
Then the son opened his mouth to ask,
  Behold fire and wood, but where is the lamb for a burnt
    offering?

In his reply, the saint spoke the rightful thing:
  The Lord will make it known who shall be His.
My son, the Master will look to His lamb
  And who is holy, He will draw to Him.

The Pure One showed him the altar of the ancients.
  A male without blemish you shall offer of your own free will.
Whispered the soft-spoken dove: Bind me as sacrifice

---

27 *shone* ṣohar = zohar.

28 Exod. 24:17.

31 *opened his mouth* idiom of Ezek. 2:8.
to ask MSS A and N point *li-sheolah*
(cf. Isa. 7:11) while B points *le-sha'alah*.
Cf. Ezek. 8:6 and Ruth 3:13.

32 Gen. 22:7.

33 Job 42:7.

34 Num. 16:5.

35 Gen. 22:8. The Holy One, blessed be
He, has appointed for Himself what is to
be His sacrifice: "The sheep for the burnt
offering—my son"; cf. Gen. R. 56:4.

36 Num. 16:5.

37 *The Pure One* The Holy One, blessed
be He (Habak. 1:13), with His finger,
as it were, pointed out to him *"the* altar"
(Gen. 22:9)—not *an* altar: which teaches

that it had been built long ago, and this
was the altar on which the earliest ones
made their offerings, Adam, Cain, Abel,
Noah and his sons. Cf. Targum Jonathan
ad Gen. 22:9, and PRE, ch. 31.

38 In the idiom of Lev. 1:3 and 22:19.

39 *soft-spoken dove yonat elem* (cf. Ps.
56:1), an epithet for Isaac, who stretched
forth his neck for slaughter like a silent
dove. Cf. Cant. R. 1:15 and beginning of
ch. 4. And see Rabbenu Ephraim in Sefer
Zekirah (NS, p. 65 = Habermann, p. 122)
who in the name of the Sifre mentions
that Israel have been compared to a
dove: "Note the dove—all other birds
when they are slaughtered shudder; but
the dove is not like that. On the contrary, it stretches forth its neck. So, there
is no one giving up his life for the sake

With cords to the horns of the altar.

Bind for me my hands and my feet
  Lest J be found wanting and profane the sacrifice.
J am afraid of panic, J am concerned to honor you,
  My will is to honor you greatly.

When the one whose life was bound up in the lad's
  Heard this, he bound him hand and foot like the perpetual
    offering.

---

of the Holy One, blessed be He, save Israel alone, as it is said, 'Yea for Thy sake are we killed' (Ps. 44:23)." In our sources, this is found in Tanhuma, Teṣawweh, 5, and Tanhuma, ed. Buber, Teṣawweh (II, p. 96), and Yalkut, Canticles, #984.

40 Ps. 118:28.

41 *Bind* Read *t'sar*, not *t'sor*: so the rhyme requires, even when the two verbs are to be pointed in *pi'el* or *niph'al*. As for the idea in lines 42-43, see the midrashic comments, that Isaac begged his father to tie him down firmly lest he be startled by the terror of the knife, and thus a blemish form in him and he be rendered unfit for an offering; or lest (in panic) his leg fly out against his father and thus he be guilty of transgressing the commandment to honor one's father. "Tie me down hand and foot . . . lest I tremble and become disqualified for sacrifice": Tanhuma, ed. Buber, I, p. 114 and parallels. See Seder Eliyahu R., ch. 25, p. 138, and Seder Eliyahu Zuta, ch. 2, p. 174: "Father, tighter, tighter bind me . . . lest I boot up and strike you, and thus become guilty of two (sins punishable by) death from heaven." And so too the poet, Solomon ibn Gabirol: "Rise

now, father, the victim tie/Lest the sword me terrify,/Fasten me down lest I the sacrifice disqualify" (see *Poems of Solomon ibn Gabirol*, ed. Bialik and Ravnitzki (Berlin and Tel Aviv, 1924-32), II, p. 167).

43 *panic bi'ut.* For the idiom cf. "Terrors shall overwhelm him" (Job 18:11). And so too in Midrash Wa-Yosha, p. 37, and Midrash Akedat Yizhak in Michael Higger's *Halakot we-Aggadot*, p. 72: "Tie down my hands and feet tighter, tighter . . . lest J panic from fear of the knife and boot you."

J am concerned (to honor) hasti. In the idiom of "being considerate of the proper respect due" (M. Hagigah 2:1). And the variant reading *hashti*, I hasten, on the basis of Eccl. 2:25 or Gen. R. 56:8 according to the reading of the regularly printed editions: "I fear lest my body tremble from fear of the knife."

44 Num. 24:11.

45 In the idiom of Gen. 44:30 and I Sam. 18:1.

46 B. Tamid 31b, and B. Shabbat 54a: hand and foot bound as was bound Isaac ben Abraham.

In their right order he prepared fire and wood,
    And offered upon them the burnt offering.

Then did the father and the son embrace,
    Mercy and Truth met and kissed each other.
Oh, my father, fill your mouth with praise,
    For He doth bless the sacrifice.

I long to open my mouth to recite the Grace:
    Forever blessed be the Lord. Amen.
Gather my ashes, bring them to the city,
    Unto the tent, to Sarah.

He made haste, he pinned him down with his knees,
    He made his two arms strong.
With steady hands he slaughtered him according to the rite,
    Full right was the slaughter.

Down upon him fell the resurrecting dew, and he revived.

---

47 PRE, ch. 31: And he set in order *the fire* and the wood (Higger version, loc. cit.), and MhG, p. 354, This teaches that he set them (i.e., the logs) the way the wood of the woodpile is set up, etc. See what I wrote at the end of ch. IV.

48 Exod. 40:29.

50 In the idiom of Ps. 85:12.

52. I Sam. 9:13.

54 Ps. 89:53.

55 Midrash Wa-Yosha, p. 37, and Yalkut, #101: Isaac said to him: Father, hurry, do the will of thy Creator . . . and burn me up thoroughly, and take my ashes, bring them to my mother Sarah, and leave them in an urn in her room. Cf. Higger's *Halakot we-Aggadot*, p. 72.

56 Gen. 18:6.

57-58 PRE, ch. 31 (cf. Higger's version, p. 195 and p. 261, n. 60) and Midrash Wa-Yosha, p. 37: He flexed his muscles (lit., he made mighty his arms) and with great force came down with his two knees on him.

59 In the idiom of Exod. 17:12.

    according to the rite be-token. In the right way, as the *halakah* requires.

60 Gen. 43:16.

61 On the model of "and the day sank down, was fast spent": Judg. 19:11. See

(The father) seized him (then) to slaughter him once more.
Scripture, bear witness! Well-grounded is the fact:
And the Lord called Abraham, even a second time from
  heaven.

The ministering angels cried out, terrified:
Even animal victims, were they ever slaughtered twice?
Instantly they made their outcry heard on high,
  Lo, Ariels cried out above the earth.

We beg of Thee, have pity upon him!
In his father's house, we were given hospitality.
He was swept by the flood of celestial tears

Lekah Tob *ad* Gen. 31:42: When Isaac underwent Akedah and his soul took wing, and the Holy One, blessed be He, restored it (to him) by means of the dew of resurrection. See above, ch. IV, on the haggadah about the Eighteen Benedictions in *Shibbole ba-Leket*, sec. 18.

63 *well-grounded is the fact la-dabar raglayim*, as the Mishnah puts it, Nazir 9:2, etc.

64 Gen. 22:15. In Scripture: *An angel of the Lord.*

66 If in slaughtering there occurs an interrupting pause long enough for a slaughtering stroke, it is disqualified; cf. B. Hullin 32a.

67 *Instantly nebisah,* note the expression (I Sam. 21:9), "because the king's business required *baste, nabus.*" And so also in his dirge ("How doth the abandoned one sit solitary"), did our rabbi put it: "At once the faithful shepherd to His angels ran. . . . In outer space, lo, Ariels screamed, to a man!"

68 Isa. 33:7, the *baftarah,* prophetic reading, for the Torah selection of Gen. 22; cf. Mann, p. 173. Gen. R. 56:5 and parallels: When Father Abraham put forth his hand to take the knife to slaughter his son, the ministering angels wept, even as it is written, "Lo, Ariels . . . angels of peace weep bitterly."

69 PRE, ch. 31 (according to the reading in Yalkut, #101 and Higger, op. cit.): The ministering angels said: Master of the universe, You have been called "Gracious and Compassionate" (Ps. 145:8); O You whose compassion is over all His works (ibid.: 9), have pity on Isaac, etc.

70 Midrash Wa-Yosha, p. 38, and Pesikta R. 171a: They kept shrieking . . . "The highways lie waste, the host for the wayfarer ceases" (Isa. 33:8): Where is the rewarding of those who extend hospitality! Cf. Gen. 18:5.

71 *He was swept hatafo = gerafo.* Note Job 9:12.

celestial the tears of the ones who dwell on high: Eccl. 5:7.

Into Eden, the garden of God.

The pure one thought: The child is free of guilt,
  Now I, whither shall I go?
Then he heard: Your son was found an acceptable sacrifice,
  By Myself have I sworn it, saith the Lord.

In a nearby thicket did the Lord prepare
A ram, meant for this mitsvah even from Creation.
The proxy caught its leg in the skirts of his coat,
  And behold, he stood by his burnt offering.

So he offered the ram, as he desired to do,

---

72 Ezek. 28:13.

73 Abraham thought: The lad is innocent before the Lord. That is to say,
when Abraham saw that Isaac had van-
ished, he feared that this happened because of his own, Abraham's, sin, that he
had not fulfilled the commandment as he
had been commanded.

74 Gen. 37:30. Abraham said before the
Holy One, blessed be He: Master of the
universe, Is it *for naught* Thou didst say
to me, "Take now your son"? Cf. Tanhuma, Shelah, 14, and Tanhuma, ed. Buber, Shelah, 27.

75 A voice (from heaven) sounded forth
and said to him: Abraham, Abraham,
"Go thy way, eat thy bread with joy.
. . . For *God hath* already *accepted* thy
works" (Eccl. 9:7), God hath accepted
thy *sacrifice.* Cf. Eccl. R., *ad loc.,* Lev.
R. 20:2.

76 Gen. 22:16.

78 As the talmudic Sages say, The ram
for Abraham's benefit was created at

twilight of the Sabbath eve of the week
of Creation: Abot 5 and B. Pesahim 54a.

79 PRE, ch. 31 (according to the Yalkut,
#101, reading, and cf. Higger, loc. cit.):
"R. Zechariah says: That ram that was
created at twilight kept running to arrive
in time to be offered up in place of Isaac.
And Samael kept preventing him in order
to undo the sacrifice of Father Abraham.
And the ram was caught in the trees by
his two horns. What did that ram do?
He reached out with his foreleg [Yalkut:
and rear leg] *for Abraham's cloak.* Abraham looked behind him and saw the ram;
he released him and offered him up." And
so too speaks R. Meir bar Isaac, the can-
tor, in the *Akedah* beginning "The covenant and the love": "That ransom, at
twilight created, got caught in the thick,/
The proxy for the favorite approached
and seized his cloak."

80 Num. 23:17.

81 *as he desired to do* Tanhuma, Shelah, 14, and Num. R. 17:2: Said Abra-

Rather than his son, as a burnt offering.
Rejoicing, he beheld the ransom of his only one
Which God delivered into his hand.

This place he called Adonai-Yireh,
The place where light and the law are manifest.
He swore to bless it as the Temple site,
For there the Lord commanded the blessing.

Thus prayed the binder and the bound,
That when their descendants commit a wrong
This act be recalled to save them from disaster,
From all their transgressions and sins.

---

ham: Master of the whole world, it is impossible for me to descend from here without offering a sacrifice. Said the Holy One, blessed be He, to him: Your sacrifice has been ready, etc. Forthwith, "And he looked, and behold, a ram": Gen. 22:13.

82 Ibid.

84 Exod. 21:13.

85 Gen. 22:14.

86 As the talmudic Sages say, Moriah—One said, for from there *hora'ah*, Torah teaching and law, goes out to the world; and the other said, for from there *orah*, light, goes out to the world; cf. J. Berakot 4, 8c, and L. Ginzberg, *Commentary on the Palestinian Talmud* (New York, 1941-61), II, pp. 404f.

87 Cf. Gen. 22:16. In Mount Moriah, the site of the Akedah, the House of the Lord was built: II Chron. 3:1.

88 Ps. 133:3.

89 So they went both of them together (Gen. 22:9), the one to sacrifice and the other to be the sacrifice; Gen. R. 56:3.

90-91 Lev. 29:9, Tanhuma, ed. Buber, Wa-Yera, 46, and Yalkut, #101: When Isaac's children are sinning before Thee, remember for their sake the Akedah of their Father Isaac, and redeem them from their distress. Cf. Targum Jonathan I and II *ad* Gen. 22:14. See also Gen. R. 56:10 and the parallels recorded above in ch. IX. In all the early sources, it is the father alone, the one who is to do the sacrificing, who prays. But in Bereshit Rabbati, p. 91: "R. Simlai said: Abraham wrapped his cloak about him in order to pray, *and also Isaac his son*. . . . Said Isaac: It is manifest before Thee that it was not an ox I offered up before Thee, but my very own flesh. So too when my children come to grief and persecutions . . . recall my Akedah to their credit, and let it appear before Thee as though my ashes were heaped up on top of the altar."

92 Lev. 16:16.

O Righteous One, do us this grace!
   You promised our fathers mercy to Abraham.
Let then their merit stand as our witness,
      And pardon our iniquity and our sin, and take us for Thine
      inheritance.

Recall to our credit the many Akedahs,
   The saints, men and women, slain for Thy sake.
Remember the righteous martyrs of Judah,
      Those that were bound of Jacob.

Be Thou the shepherd of the surviving flock
   Scattered and dispersed among the nations.
Break the yoke and snap the bands
      Of the bound flock that yearns toward Thee

   O GOD! O KING . . .

94 Micah 7:20.

95 Gen. 30:33; Deut. 8:15.

96 Exod. 34:9.

98 Ps. 44:23.

99 Gen. 30:28 and 39.

100 Ibid. 30:42; and this expression was made to refer to those slain for the Sanctification of the Name.

101 Gen. 30:36.

102 Esth. 3:8.

103 Perhaps one should vocalize *u-shevor* (break; rather than, *we-shabber*) in accordance with Jer. 30:8.

104 Gen. 30:41. In MS A, pointing *be-kol* (with *holem*, rather than with *qames*) may perhaps be explained on the basis of Cant. R. 7:11: Israel's only yearning is for their Father who is in heaven, as it said, "I am My beloved's, and his

yearning is toward Me." Or perhaps the verb *yahem* in this line is transitive; cf. MhG, p. 545: Come, see how great was the strength given to Father Jacob, of a quality of that Power on High, for he could bring the flock to heat as he wished. So too Mishnat Rabbi Eliezer, VIII, p. 150: Jacob was given the power to bring the flock to heat the way he wished. If this be the case, then perhaps the poet's meaning is: Increase their seed, and for them break through a clearance like that of the World to Come; cf. Gen. R. 73:11.

105 *O GOD! O KING EL MELEK*, seated on the Mercy Throne, etc. But possibly what the poet intends is (not El = God, but) *el*, "to"—and so lines 104f. would read, "the flock that's tied *to* the KING," etc., in the language of cleaving to the Holy One, blessed be He.

INDEX OF BIBLICAL REFERENCES

Hebrew Bible

GENESIS

3:5 . . . . 83*n*.

9:6 104

10:9 . . . . 68*n*.

15:1 115

16:12 . . . . . . 144*n*.

17:21 93

18:5 . . . . 149*n*.

18:6 . . . . 148*n*.

18:10 . . . . . . 127*n*.

18:17 . . . . . . 117*n*.

18:27 42

21:12 . . . . . . 38, 69*n*., 93*n*.

22 . . . . x, xiii, xiv, xvii, 105*n*., 149*n*.

22:1 . . . . 11*n*., 105, 109*n*., 118*n*.,144*n*.,145*n*.

22:1-5 125

22:1-10 122

22:1-13 . . . . . 124, 124*n*.

22:1-19 xi

22:2 . . . . 72*n*., 117*n*., 143*n*., 144*n*.

22:3 . . . . 11*n*., 62*n*., 114, 144*n*.

22:4 . . . . 49, 110

22:5 . . . . 5*n*., 110

22:6 . . . . 10*n*., 77

22:6-8 . . . . . . 3, 125

22:7 . . . . 49, 146*n*.

22:8 . . . . 4*n*., 10*n*., 41*n*., 43, 49, 49*n*., 52, 146*n*.

22:9 . . . . 21*n*., 36, 36*n*., 108, 125, 146*n*., 151*n*.

22:10 . . . . . . 45, 117*n*., 125

22:11 . . . . . . 123*n*., 125, 126

22:11-19 122

22:12 . . . . . . 8, 8*n*., 31*n*., 45, 45*n*., 46, 46*n*,. 83*n*., 121*n*., 123*n*., 125, 127*n*.

22:13 . . . . . . 39*n*., 40*n*., 60, 61, 61*n*., 68*n*., 78, 98, 125, 151*n*.

22:14 . . . . 42*n*., 52, 55*n*., 60,
67*n*., 93, 95*n*.,
121, 123*n*., 125,
127, 151*n*.

22:14-18 . . . . . 124, 124*n*.

22:15 . . . . . . 67, 123, 125, 126,
126*n*., 127, 149*n*.

22:15-18 . . . . . 123*n*., 124*n*.

22:15-19 125

22:16 . . . . 55, 83*n*., 91*n*.,
127, 150*n*., 151*n*.

22:16-18 . . . . . xiii*n*.

22:19 . . . . xviii, 3, 4*n*., 5*n*.,
7*n*., 8*n*., 41*n*., 47,
124, 124*n*.

23:2 . . . . 4*n*.

24 5

24:62 . . . . 6, 7

24:63 . . . . 6, 68*n*.

24:64 . . . . 6, 6*n*.

25:27 . . . . 7*n*.

26:2 . . . . 100*n*.

27:1 . . . . 31*n*.

27:20 . . . . 68*n*.

27:33 31

27:40 101

30:28 . . . . 152*n*.

30:33 . . . . 152*n*.

30:36 . . . . 152*n*.

30:39 . . . . 152*n*.

30:41 . . . . 152*n*.

30:42 . . . . 152*n*.

31:42 . . . . 32, 149*n*.

31:53 32

32:3 43

37:30 . . . . 150*n*.

39:12 114

41:9 . . . . 143*n*.

43:16 . . . . 148*n*.

44:20 . . . . 143*n*.

44:30 . . . . 147*n*.

EXODUS

4:2 . . . . 83*n*.

4:13 46

4:22 101

6:2 . . . . 46, 47*n*.

12:2 . . . . 54*n*.

12:23 . . . . . . 51, 51*n*.

14:15 . . . . . . 114*n*.

14:21 114

15:11 . . . . . . 94*n*.

17:12 . . . . . . 148*n*.

19:13 . . . . . . 38*n*., 39

19:16 110

21:13 . . . . . . 151*n*.

22:8 121

22:28 . . . . . . 54*n*.

23:15 . . . . . . 54*n*.

24:1 110

27:17 . . . . . . 146*n*.

28:41 . . . . . . 143*n*.

31:1 . . . . 54*n*.

34:6 . . . . x*n*., 121

34:9 . . . . 152*n*.

34:22 . . . . . . 54*n*.

40:29 . . . . . . 148*n*.

LEVITICUS

1:3 . . . . 146n.
1:7 36
1:9 39
1:11 73
1:15 . . . . . . 144n.
9:3 . . . . 85n.
16:16 . . . . . . 151n.
22:19 . . . . . . 146n.
22:27 . . . . . . 85n.
23:24 55
26:42 . . . . . . 41, 42n.
27:10 69
29:9 . . . . 151n.

NUMBERS

3:12 . . . . 54n.
10:10 76
16:5 . . . . 146n.
23:17 . . . . . . 150n.
23:19 . . . . . . 83n.
24:11 . . . . . . 147n.
29:1 . . . . 74n., 75n.

DEUTERONOMY

1:9 . . . . 67n.
8:15 . . . . . . 152n.
12:19 xxv
16:16 . . . . . . 67, 67n.
26 . . . . 14n., 15n.
30 . . . . 19n.
33:28 . . . . . . 20n.

JOSHUA

5:2 . . . . 123n., 126n.

JUDGES

5:28 . . . . . . 74n.
11:31 . . . . . . 68n.
14:3 . . . . 143n.
19:11 . . . . . . 148n.
19:30 . . . . . . 94n.

I SAMUEL

2:30 . . . . . . 117n.
9:13 . . . . 148n.
10:12 . . . . . . 68n.
18:1 . . . . 148n.
19:24 . . . . . . 68n.
21:9 . . . . 149n.

II SAMUEL

1:23 23
19:31 . . . . . . 144n.

I KINGS

8:14 ff. . . . . . 54n.
9:3 . . . . 70n.

II KINGS

3:27 . . . . . . 78n., 79, 80, 81n.
15:7 61

ISAIAH

5:30 . . . . 20n.
7:11 . . . . 146n.
14:13 73

17:7 . . . . 145n.
17:10 . . . . . . 118, 118n.
26:19 32
27:13 . . . . . . 39n., 110
31:5 52
33 130
33:7 . . . . 149n.
33:8 . . . . 149n.
35:8 . . . . 110n.
41:24 . . . . . . 75n.
54:10 . . . . . . 116n.
63:16 . . . . . . 101, 102
64:3 . . . . 97n.

JEREMIAH
11:15 . . . . . . 143n.
19:5 79
20:12 . . . . . . 143n.
20:16 . . . . . . 74n.
30:8 . . . . 152n.

EZEKIEL
2:8 . . . . 146n.
8:6 . . . . 146n.
9 52
28:13 . . . . . . 150n.
44:2 ff. . . . . . . xvn.

HOSEA
6:2 . . . . 109, 110n., 113

JOEL
2:13 x

AMOS
2:1 . . . . 81n.

JONAH
4:2 . . . . xn.

MICAH
6:6 f. 56
6:7 78
7:15 56
7:20 . . . . . . 152n.

NAHUM
1:10 116

HABAKKUK
1:13 . . . . . . 146n.

ZECHARIAH
3:3 108
9:14 . . . . . . 98, 98n., 99
9:15 99

PSALMS
3:4 29
8 . . . . 117n., 120n.
8:6 . . . . 117n.
11:5 . . . . . . 144n.
22:21 72
26:1 104
26:11 . . . . . . 145n.
30:9 . . . . 84n.
33:1 137
38:14 . . . . . . 91n., 94

38:14-15 . . . . . 94n.

44:23 . . . . 147n., 152n.

47:6 . . . . 89, 121

50:23 22

56:1 . . . . 146n.

79:11 . . . . . . 46, 47, 111

81:4 92

85:12 . . . . 148n.

88:6 . . . . 97n.

89:9 . . . . 94n.

89:53 . . . . . . 148n.

102:21 . . . . . . 48, 111

110:3 f. . . . . . . 33n.

110:6 . . . . 26n.

114:3 114

118:28 . . . . . . 147n.

119 . . . . 93n.

126:6 . . . . 94n.

133:3 . . . . 33, 151n.

139:4 . . . . 145n.

139:12 51

142:5 . . . . 143n.

145:8 . . . . xn., 149n.

145:9 . . . . 149n.

PROVERBS

16:1 . . . . 68n.

23:35 . . . . . . 136n.

JOB

1:6 . . . . 145n.

2:1 . . . . 145n.

2:4 . . . . 106n.

4:1 105

4:2 . . . . 145n.

4:4 106

4:5 106

4:6 106

6:5 . . . . 144n.

9:12 . . . . 149n.

18:11 . . . . . . 147n.

42:7 . . . . 146n.

CANTICLES (SONG OF SONGS)

1:13 . . . . 115n.

1:14 114

4:9 7

7:14 73

RUTH

2:10 . . . . 143n.

3:13 . . . . 146n.

ECCLESIASTES

2:25 . . . . 147n.

4:8 . . . . 83n.

5:7 . . . . 149n.

9:7 . . . . 75n., 150n.

12:6 . . . . 112n.

ESTHER

1:8 . . . . 145n.

3:8 . . . . 152n.

5:1 . . . . 95n.

DANIEL

2:22 51

8 . . . . xiiin.

I CHRONICLES   **II CHRONICLES**
   21:15 . . . . 43, 51, 52, 58   3:1 . . . . 151*n.*

Apocrypha and Pseudepigrapha

II MACCABEES   **BOOK OF JUBILEES**
   2:23-28 . . . . . 13*n.*   17:16 . . . . 108*n.*
   6 . . . . 13*n.*   17:16 f. . . . . . 107*n.*
   7 . . . . 13*n.*   18:9 . . . . 107*n.*
                                             18:12 . . . . 107*n.*
IV MACCABEES   18:18-19 . . . . . 56*n.*
   5:4 ff. . . . . . . 13*n.*
   8:3 ff. . . . . . . 13*n.*

New Testament

MATTHEW   3:25 . . . . 82*n.*
   17:23 . . . . 109*n.*   3:28 . . . . 83*n.*
                                             4:18-25 . . . . . 82*n.*
LUKE   5:8 . . . . 82*n.*
   24:7 . . . . 109*n.*   5:9 . . . . 85*n.*
                                             5:12 . . . . 82*n.*
JOHN   5:18-19 . . . . 82*n.*
   1:29 . . . . 85*n.*   6:2-11 . . . . . 83*n.*
                                             7:1-7 . . . . . . 83*n.*
ACTS OF THE APOSTLES   7:1-6 . . . . . 97*n.*
   13:34 . . . . 83*n.*   8:32 . . . . 82*n.*, 83*n.*
   13:39 . . . . 83*n.*   9:7 . . . . 82*n.*
   18:3 . . . . 81*n.*

                                          I CORINTHIANS
ROMANS   2:9 . . . . 97*n.*
   3:23-26 . . . . . 82*n.*   5:7 . . . . 85*n.*

15:4 . . . . 82*n.*, 109*n.*
15:20-21 . . . . . 82*n.*
15:27 . . *.* . . . . 117*n.*
15:45-49 . . . . . 82*n.*

II CORINTHIANS
4:4 . . . . 108*n.*
5:21 . . . . 84*n.*

GALATIANS
1:4 . . . . 82*n.*
3:8 . . . . 82*n.*
3:10-13 . . . . . 83*n.*
3:13-14 . . . . . 82*n.*
4:28 . . . . 82*n.*

EPHESIANS
2:2 . . . . 108*n.*
6:12 . . . . 108*n.*

COLOSSIANS
1:15-18 . . . . . 82*n.*

I THESSALONIANS
5:10 . . . . 83*n.*

HEBREWS
2:14 . . . . 104*n.*
11:17-19 . . . . . 19*n.*

REVELATION OF JOHN
5:6-9 . . . . . . 85*n.*

INDEX OF MIDRASHIC-TALMUDIC SAGES

Abba, 92
Abbahu, 76, 76n., 83n., 100
Abin, 83n., 84n.
Aha bar Jacob, 96n., 109
Akiba, 96n.

Benaiah, 61, 62, 63, 66
Berekiah, 4, 55, 92n., 93n., 110n., 115n., 124n.
Berekiah bar Abba, 93n.
Berekiah, ha-kohen, 92, 93n.
Bibi bar Abba, 90, 91, 95, 100

Eleazar ben Pedat, 3, 41, 43, 105
Eliezer, 31n., 40, 55, 97n.

Hanina (Haninah) ben Dosa of Sepphoris, 39, 43, 81n., 100, 105
Hilkiah, 83n., 84n.
Hillel, 136
Hinnanah (Hinanah, Hinnana) bar Isaac, 92, 98n.-99n., 115
Huna, 97n.
Huna bar Issac, 99n.
Hiyya bar Abba, 97n.
Hoshaya, 100, 105

Isaac, 40, 110
Isaac Napha, 43, 44, 110, 110n.

Ishmael ben Elisha, 51, 89, 123n.

Jacob of Kefar Hanan, 33n.
Jeremiah, 93n.
Johanan ben Nuri, 3, 44, 68n., 87, 90, 91, 92, 93n., 95, 96, 96n., 97, 97n., 100, 105, 106, 108, 109, 109n., 110, 143n.
Jonathan, 100, 101
Joseph, 96n.
Joshua, 40, 55, 111
Joshua ben Hananiah, 50
Joshua of Siknin, 78n.
Josiah, 38n.
Judah, 30, 40, 117n.
Judah bar Nahmani, 89
Judah bar Simon, 98n.
Judah the Prince, 48, 100, 105
Judan bar Shalom, 98n.

Levi bar Hama, 43, 92, 98, 108, 109, 110

Nehemiah, 90n.

Pinhas, 61
Pinhas ha-kohen bar Hama, 84n.

Rabbi, see Judah the Prince
Rabbah bar Isaac, 123n.

Resh Lakish, 33n., 68n., 104n.; *see also* Simeon ben Lakish

Samuel, 40
Samuel bar Isaac, 96n.
Samuel bar Nahman (Nahmani), 42, 101, 121n.
Shila, 66n.
Simeon bar Abba, 143n.
Simeon ben Eleazar, 117n., 145n.
Simeon ben Lakish, 106; *see also* Resh Lakish
Simeon ben Menasia, 117n.

Simeon ben Yohai, 50, 106

Yelamdenu, 26n., 47n., 75n., 77n., 91n., 93n., 126n., 144n.
Yose, 40, 96n., 97n.
Yose bar Halafta, 101
Yose bar Haninah, 3
Yose ben Zimrah, 48, 105, 108, 109n.
Yudan, 61
Yudan son of Manasseh, 42

Zechariah, 150n.

EPHRAIM OF BONN

Ephraim of Bonn, ix, xi, xiv, xv, xxvi, 17n., 21n., 26, 26n., 129, 130, 130n., 131, 136, 137, 144n.